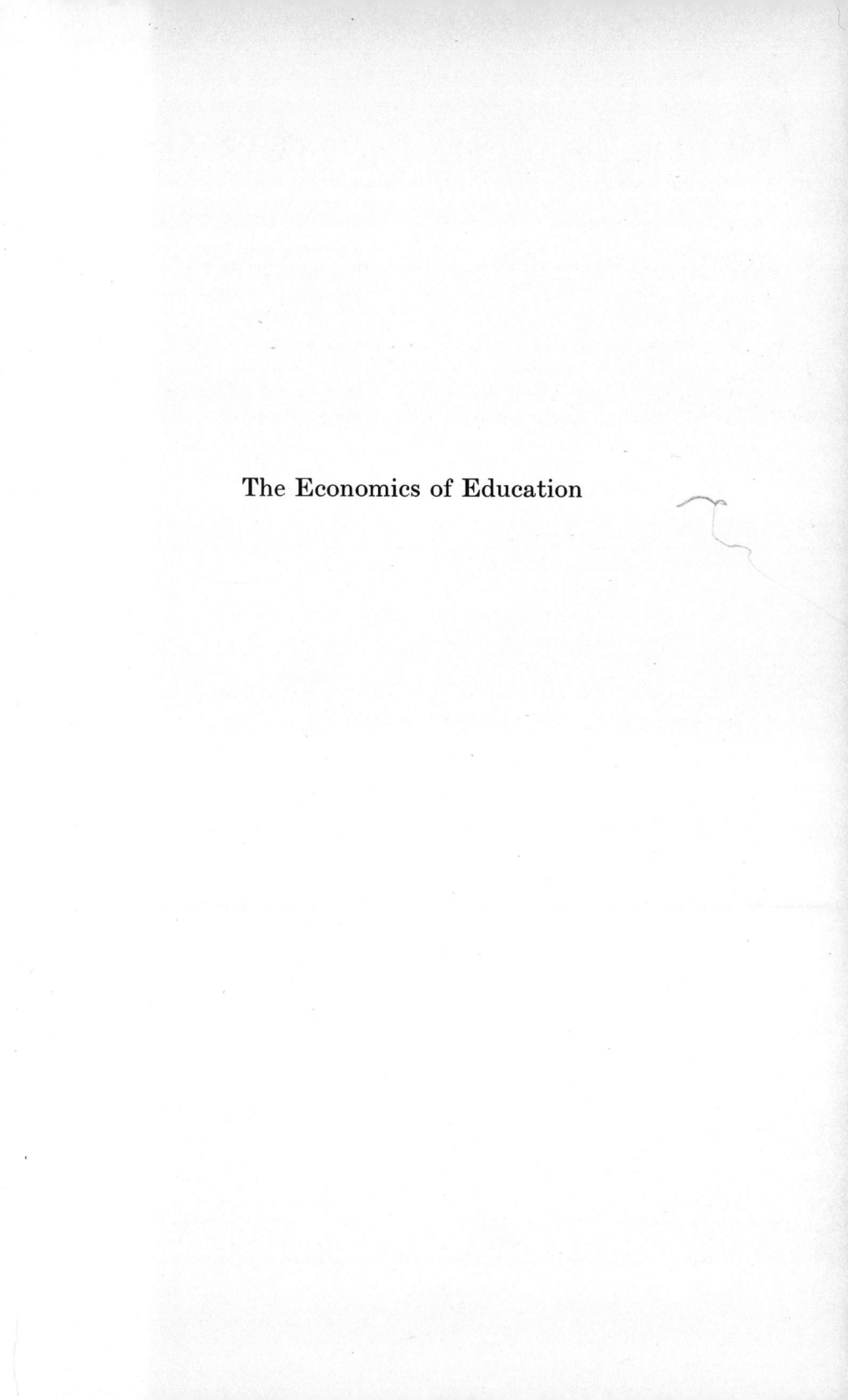

The Economics of Education

THE PROFESSIONAL EDUCATION SERIES

Walter K. Beggs, *Editor*
Dean Emeritus
Teachers College
University of Nebraska

Royce H. Knapp, *Research Editor*
Regents Professor of Education
Teachers College
University of Nebraska

The Economics of Education

by

LOUIS J. RODRIGUEZ
Vice President for Academic Affairs
University of Texas at San Antonio

and

DEWEY D. DAVIS
Professor of Education
University of Texas at San Antonio

PROFESSIONAL EDUCATORS PUBLICATIONS, INC.
LINCOLN, NEBRASKA

To
Ramona and Ruth

Library of Congress Catalog Card No.: 73-86207

ISBN 0-88224-059-5

© Copyright 1974
by
Professional Educators Publications, Inc.

All Rights Reserved

PRINTED IN U.S.A.

Contents

INTRODUCTION 9

1. EDUCATIONAL EXPANSION IN THE UNITED STATES 10

   Milestones in Expanding Educational Opportunities for Colonial America 10
   States Assume Responsibility for Education 11
   Financing Educational Expansion 12
   Comparative Guide of State Expenditures 15
   Expenditures in Higher Education 18
   Current Status of Education Financing and Enrollment . . . 19
   Public Concerns with Education 21
   Economic Principles Related to Education 22

2. ECONOMIC CONTRIBUTIONS OF EDUCATION 28

   Productivity 28
   Economic Growth and Education 34
   Areas of Investment 38
   Summary 46

3. DEMAND FOR EDUCATION 48

   Demographic Factors Influencing Demand 48
   Race and Ethnic Factors 51
   Literacy a Factor in Educational Demand 53
   Income Related to Educational Demand 54
   Migration and Its Effect on Higher Education 55
   Ability and Its Relationship to Obtaining Advanced Degrees . 59

State Population Related to Demand for College Degrees . . 59
NDEA Title IV Graduate Fellowships Awarded, by Geographic Location 61
Population Trends in Metropolitan Centers Affecting Educational Demand 62
Employment as an Educational Demand 63
Geographic Location Related to Years of Schooling Completed 63
Governmental Regulations and Educational Demand . . . 63
Summary 67

4. SUPPLY OF EDUCATIONAL SERVICES 69

Costs of Providing Education 69
Capital 73
Equipment 75
Materials 76
Obsolescence 77
Inflation and Interest 78
Societal Opportunity Costs 81
Marketing of Education 81
Accessibility 82
Sale Price of Education 83

5. MARKET VERSUS PUBLIC SOLUTIONS TO THE PROBLEMS OF FINANCING EDUCATION 86

Market and Public Concepts 86
Market Solution 89
Public Solution 91
Economic Principles and Education 110
Summary and Conclusions 111

6. SUMMARY AND CONCLUSIONS 114

Tables

Chapter 1

1.1	Increase in Overall and Per Pupil Expenditures, 1889–1972	13
1.2	Increase in Earned Degrees, 1889–1972	13
1.3	Financing Higher Education, 1966–67	14
1.4	Percentage of Population in Various Age Groups, 1971	16
1.5	Effect of Migration on State Income	17
1.6	Rising Educational Expenditures, 1930–70	19

Chapter 2

2.1	Output Per Man-Hour, Hourly Compensation, and Unit-Labor Costs in the Private Economy, 1950–70	33
2.2	Population, Labor Force, Employment, and Unemployment, 1950–72	40
2.3	Percentage of Labor Force Unemployed, 1955–72	42
2.4	Years of School Completed, by Race and Age, 1970	43
2.5	Employment Status of High School Graduates and School Dropouts, 1965–70	44
2.6	Occupations and Educational Levels of Employed Persons, 1959 and 1970	45

Chapter 3

3.1	Educational Enrollments, by Level and Type of Institution, 1970	49
3.2	Regional Variations in School Enrollments	49
3.3	Years of School Completed, by Sex	50
3.4	Median Scores on Achievement Tests of Grade-1 and Grade-12 Students, 1965	52
3.5	Illiteracy, by Age and Race	53

3.6	Median Income and Educational Attainments of Men Aged 25–54	54
3.7	Students Moving from State to State for Higher Education, 1958–68	56
3.8	College-Age Students Enrolled in Selected States, 1968	57
3.9	Increase in Number of Earned Advanced Degrees, 1949–70	58
3.10	Earned Advanced Degrees, 1949–70, by Sex	58
3.11	Relationship Between State Population and Number of Residents Obtaining Advanced Degrees	60
3.12	Distribution of NDEA Title IV Graduate Fellowships, 1970	61
3.13	Decreasing Number of Whites Living in Urban Centers, 1900–70	62
3.14	Unemployment Among High School Graduates and Dropouts Aged 16–21	64
3.15	Some Examples of Federal Support for Education, Fiscal 1972	66

CHAPTER 4

4.1	Utilization of Public School (K–12) Funds, 1963–64	71
4.2	Utilization of Higher Education Funds, 1950–68	72
4.3	Capital Outlay Expenditures by School Systems, 1959–70	74
4.4	Interest Payments on Public School (K–12) Debt, 1961–70	80
4.5	Interest Rates on School Bonds, 1963–70	80

CHAPTER 5

5.1	Amount and Source of Public and Private School Expenditures, 1960–71	93
5.2	Control and Level of Instruction of Public and Private School Expenditures, 1930–71	95
5.3	Revenues and Expenditures of Public Elementary and Secondary Schools, 1950–68	96
5.4	New Bond Sales for Public School Purposes, 1968–70	98
5.5	Estimated Public School Expenditures, 1971, and Personal Income, 1969, by State	99
5.6	State Appropriations for Education, 1962–72	103
5.7	Federal Work and Training Programs, 1963–70	104
5.8	Federal Funds for Education and Related Activities, 1966–71	105
5.9	Federally Aided Vocational Programs, 1950–69	109

Introduction

The United States in recent years has experienced a profound increase in concern with the economic dimensions of education. Educators, legislators, taxpayers, and buyers of educational services have become much more aware of cost factors in education. Economic education programs, coordinated by organizations such as the Joint Council on Economic Education and various state councils, with the support of a combination of industry, labor, and professional groups, have mushroomed during the past decade. However, one of the areas often neglected in high school and basic college-level undergraduate economic education is the subject of the economics of education. This situation exists at a time when the financing of education in our country is assuming the dimensions of a major problem area. Furthermore, the average American taxpayer and legislator have a paucity of factual material to shed some light on this problem.

The purpose of this text is to examine the economics of education as it exists in the United States. Organizationally, the text: (1) presents a very brief introduction on the history of the financing of education; (2) examines the patterns of educational expenditures during 1960–73; (3) describes the current financial status of education; (4) evaluates the contribution of education to productivity and economic growth; (5) presents and reviews the demand for education as it relates to demographic and economic factors; (6) examines the supply of educational services as they relate to production costs and marketing; and (7) evaluates alternative solutions to the problem of financing education. Our hope is that this material will be useful to students, educators, legislators, and taxpayers.

We are indebted to the University of Texas at San Antonio for helping to make this project possible. Specifically, Mrs. Nelda Walls, Mrs. Sylvia Zavaleta, and Mrs. Sonya Masinter of UTSA worked diligently to type the various drafts of the manuscript. The idea for this book originated at the annual meeting of the Joint Council on Economic Education in 1971.

CHAPTER 1

Educational Expansion in the United States

When one examines the history of education in the United States, a chronicle of continuous expansion is noted in nearly every facet. One striking exception to this generalization is the decrease in the number of schools and school districts over the last three decades as a result of consolidation. All the various forms of expansion are punctuated with economic overtones. A brief review of significant milestones in the history of public education in the United States will substantiate this generalization.

MILESTONES IN EXPANDING EDUCATIONAL OPPORTUNITIES FOR COLONIAL AMERICA

Harvard College was founded in 1636 to meet a demand for increasing the literacy of the clergy and to operate as an agency for social change. The Boston Latin Grammar School was established the same year to assure that a larger number of youth might be prepared for beginning studies in the learned professions. The Massachusetts Law of 1642 required compulsory education of children and assigned responsibility for it to parents. This precipitated the "Old Deluder Satan" Law of 1647, which stipulated that all towns of fifty or more families must provide a master to teach their children. Towns with a hundred or more families were required to maintain a grammar school to prepare children for college.[1] In the early history of this country the majority of southern slave-owners provided education for their charges, who as a result developed into a more valuable work force. Because this made exploitation more difficult, the practice was largely discontinued by the beginning of the nineteenth century.

1. George F. Kneller, *Foundations of Education* (New York: John Wiley & Sons, 1967), pp. 5, 6.

Progress in making public education more widely available continued during the first seventy-five years of the eighteenth century. A severe setback is noted during the Revolutionary War, but shortly after England's recognition of American sovereignty Congress passed the famous Land Ordinance of 1785 and the Northwest Ordinance of 1787. These ordinances imparted an early and significant impetus to free public education. Financing was provided through sporadic efforts and philanthropic contributions rather than a broad-based taxation. Although no statewide system of elementary or secondary education had come into existence by 1800, all the states had statewide systems a century later. The last hope for providing a system of public education without compulsory public support was the monitorial system of education enthusiastically heralded by Joseph Lancaster. It was supposed to provide efficient and cheap free schools, but it did not live up to its claims. The balance of the nineteenth century was a period in which the states and municipalities increasingly called upon their citizenries to support free public education by taxing themselves.

STATES ASSUME RESPONSIBILITY FOR EDUCATION

Massive immigration to the United States, the economic value of large families, and improvement in medical services all contributed to a substantial population boom. Because the expanding economy required a better-educated labor force, the trend toward more formal education began. It is still with us today. The increase in students necessitated employing more teachers and the Massachusetts Legislature met this demand by creating the first public normal school in 1838 at Lexington, the cradle of the Revolution. It was the first of a new species of teacher-training institution that was to become very widely available throughout the country.

The Kalamazoo Decision of 1874 by the Michigan Supreme Court firmly established a legal basis for secondary education. Subsequent to this decision there was a rapid expansion of secondary education throughout the country. More people became qualified for college-level studies, and society moved to meet this challenge.

The twentieth century has witnessed the creation of two additional types of institution to cope with educational expansion. The community junior college, the only uniquely American institution of education, has placed higher education both geographically and financially within easy reach of the vast majority of the population of this country. Its growth in numbers, size, and importance since World War II has been spectacular.

Much additional information on this exciting institution is available in a book by Dr. James W. Reynolds.[2]

The second type of institution resulting from this expansion, which will also probably have an enormous effect on our society, is the multicampus university system. Many state universities were purposely established in small, isolated towns so students would not be subjected to the temptations and distractions of life in metropolitan areas. This was consistent with the philosophy that an education necessitates reflective and introspective efforts by the learner. Today many feel that a better education results from immersing the learner in the activities of a dynamic society. People in metropolitan areas have pressured legislatures to create state universities where people live and where the action is. Examples of such institutions are Louisiana State University at New Orleans, the University of Texas at San Antonio, the University of Colorado at Denver, the State University of New York at Buffalo, Florida International University of Miami, the University of Alabama at Birmingham, and the University of Wisconsin at Milwaukee. Many of these extensions will become larger and perhaps more influential than the parent campuses. The multicampus university will certainly be an exciting institution to study during the last quarter of the twentieth century. It represents the newest entry in the chronicle of educational expansion dealt with in this introduction.

FINANCING EDUCATIONAL EXPANSION

Generally, the willingness of the populace to pay for the education they requested increased proportionately until 1960. Since then the demand for education has increased but so has a reluctance to pay for it. Just as private citizens turned to states and towns for financial assistance during the formative years of our public educational system, so today one sees increasing demands for federal financial support. This has caused many to ask if our expanding educational effort is moving us toward expanding federal control of the system.

The economic investment in education has continued to rise because America has chosen to educate an increasingly larger percentage of its population each year and to spend more on the education of each individual. Table 1.1 shows these trends clearly. Even when provision is made for inflation, with the accompanying decrease in the purchasing power of the dollar, the true expenditures have substantially increased. This has

---

2. James W. Reynolds, *The Comprehensive Junior College Curriculum* (Berkeley: McCutchan Publishing Corp., 1969).

TABLE 1.1

INCREASE IN OVERALL AND PER PUPIL EXPENDITURES, 1889–1972

School Year	Number of 17-yr.-olds	H.S. Graduates[a]	Total Expenditures[b]	Per Pupil Expenditure
1889–90 . .	1,259,177	3.5	NAD[c]	NAD[c]
1949–50 . .	2,034,450	59.0	5,838	$ 259
1959–60 . .	2,862,005	65.1	15,613	472
1971–72 . .	3,961,000	76.8	48,600	1,144

[a] Percentage of total.   [b] In millions of dollars.   [c] NAD = No accurate data.

SOURCE: *The Official Associated Press Almanac, 1973* (New York: Almanac Publishing Co., 1972), p. 374.

resulted in better educational programs headed by increasingly more competent professionals.

The data given in Table 1.2 are a testimonial to the expansion of education in this country. They demonstrate that there has been a steady increase in the amount of people earning baccalaureate and other advanced degrees. Superficially, 1949–50 might appear to be an exception to this trend, since fewer degrees were earned in the period following, but this is because 1949–50 was a "bumper" year for degree-granting due to the large number of World War II veterans who had invaded college campuses in 1945, 1946, and 1947.

Approximately 10 percent of the gross national product of the United States is accounted for by the cost of formal education. This certainly indicates that education makes an enormous direct, as well as indirect,

TABLE 1.2

INCREASE IN EARNED DEGREES, 1889–1972

Year	Degrees Awarded	Bachelor	Master	Doctor
1889–90 . . .	16,703	15,539	1,015	149
1949–50 . . .	496,661	432,058	58,183	6,420
1954–60 . . .	476,704	392,440	74,435	9,829
1971–72 . . .	1,175,000	903,000	237,900	34,700

SOURCE: *The Official Associated Press Almanac, 1973* (New York: Almanac Publishing Co., 1972), p. 374.

impact on the economy of the nation. About one-third of the expenditure is for higher education and two-thirds for kindergarten through twelfth grade (K–12) education. Most of the costs of K–12 education are borne by local and state governments while higher education has a more varied base of economic support.

Support for higher education is broken down for the year 1966–67 in Table 1.3. The total expenditure for higher education that year was $16.8 billion. Assuming that most people wanting work during that year could have found it, we must add to the cost of formal education the wages students might have earned if they had been employed in the economy rather than acquiring an education. This would probably have amounted to over $15 billion. The public deserves an accounting of how carefully such a large investment is utilized.

A wealthy state in this country may spend over two times as much per student on public education as a poor state. Yet the efforts made by the citizens of the poor state may be as great or greater than those by the citizens of the wealthy state. One might question why such an inequity of opportunity for children has continued to exist for over a century. The answer ultimately must deal with the selfishness of individual states.

To date it has been politically impossible to pass a major bill dealing with federal contributions to education in individual states that would directly benefit one group of states and exclude others. Even though many enlightened Congressmen and at least two Presidents have attempted to cope with this financial inequity, they have not been able to get a corrective legislative measure through the House of Representatives and the Senate. In August, 1946, Senator Robert Taft, one of our most famous political leaders, added his considerable influence to this cause by suggesting that

TABLE 1.3

FINANCING HIGHER EDUCATION, 1966–67

Sources of Income	Percentage of Total
Donations and Institutional Earnings	35.1
State Governments	23.8
Federal Government	22.6
Student Tuition and Fees	16.1
Local Governments	2.4

SOURCE: Charles S. Benson, *The Economics of Public Education* (New York: Houghton Mifflin Co., 1968), p. 11.

the federal government had a responsibility to see that every child in the country received at least the minimum education necessary in order to avail himself of the opportunities promised by the American dream.[3] On at least two occasions equalization-of-opportunity bills easily cleared the Senate but were killed in the House of Representatives.

Bringing the twenty states most in need of equalization to within 80 percent of the average expenditure per student for the nation would not require a huge federal expenditure since, except for Texas, these are mainly states with relatively small populations. However, in order to gain the political support necessary for passage, the bills are amended and changed until the wealthier states are also included in the expenditure. When this is done the cost becomes quite prohibitive and the inequity continues to exist in almost the same ratio. Additional information on this topic can be found in the book by Charles S. Benson cited in note 3.

COMPARATIVE GUIDE OF STATE EXPENDITURES

At least two variables must be evaluated in attempting to examine the effort a state makes in financing education: the per capita income of the state, and the percentage of that income being used to provide educational opportunities. It would also be wise to investigate the percentage of the population in various age brackets; for example, 0–4 preschool, 5–12 elementary-school age, 13–18 secondary-school age, and 18–22 college age. Keeping in mind that the same quality of education can be purchased cheaper in some states than in others, the ability of states to finance education varies dramatically.

In 1971, Connecticut, New York, Nevada, New Jersey, and Hawaii had an average per capita income of $4,915, while Mississippi, Arkansas, Alabama, South Carolina, and Virginia had an average per capita income of only $3,048, or about 62 percent of that of the wealthier states. If 5 percent of the per capita income is earmarked for financing a suitable level of education in the wealthier states, then the poorer states would have to utilize about 8.1 percent of their per capita income to provide the same amount of money for educating each member of their citizenry who avails himself of such service. Historically, the problem has been compounded by the emigration of productive-aged people from the poor to the wealthier states, thereby leaving a larger percentage of nonproductive school-age people in the poorer states. The data in Table 1.4 are an elaboration of this problem.

3. Charles S. Benson, *The Economics of Public Education* (New York: Houghton Mifflin Co., 1968), p. 11.

TABLE 1.4

Percentage of Population in Various Age Groups, 1971

Age Group	Description	Percentage of Total
0–22	Education Liability	43.8
23–64	Economically Productive	45.8
over 65	Fixed Income	10.4

Source: *Statistical Abstract of the United States: 1971.* The data in the table were synthesized from selected papers in the cited reference.

In order to illustrate how this problem is compounded, Table 1.5 represents the situation in two hypothetical states signified by ws (wealthy state with per capita income of $5,000) and ps (poor state with per capita income of $3,000). Assume the fixed-income groups have a per capita income equal to the state average and then compute money that would be produced by supporting education on the basis of 5 percent of the income before and after migration of productive-aged population. Also assume that the productive-aged group must generate all the income that is given for the education-liability group in average per capita income. This means that productive-aged people in the wealthy state average $9,782 per capita and in the poor state $5,867 per capita.

Income for schools in wealthier states would be increased by productive people moving into the state while income for schools in poorer states would be decreased by loss of earnings of productive-aged workers leaving the state.

Income for Wealthy-State Schools

$IWS = 0.05 \ (4,000,000) \ (\$5,000) + (0.05) \ 0.2(1,832,000) \ (\$9,982)$

$IWS = \$1,000,000,000 + \$179,000,000$

$IWS = \$1,179,000,000$

Income for Poor-State Schools

$IPS = 0.05 \ (4,000,000) \ (\$3,000) - (0.05) \ 0.2(1,832,000) \ (\$5,867)$

$IPS = \$600,000,000 - \$107,000,000$

$IPS = \$493,000,000$

From the preceding argument one might think that the way to insure a child a quality education would be to move to one of the wealthier states, but this is not the case. Frequently the citizenry of the poorer states are willing to tax themselves at a much higher rate, realizing that an

TABLE 1.5
EFFECT OF MIGRATION ON STATE INCOME

<table>
<tr><th rowspan="3">Age Group</th><th colspan="4">BEFORE MIGRATION</th><th colspan="4">AFTER MIGRATION</th></tr>
<tr><th colspan="2">Population (In Thousands)</th><th colspan="2">Money Produced By 5 Percent of Income (In Millions of Dollars)</th><th colspan="2">Dollars Available Per Person 0–22 Years</th><th colspan="2">Population (In Thousands)</th><th colspan="2">Money Produced By 5 Percent of Income (In Millions of Dollars)</th><th colspan="2">Dollars Available Per Person 0–22 Years</th></tr>
<tr><th>PS</th><th>WS</th><th>PS</th><th>WS</th><th>PS</th><th>WS</th><th>PS</th><th>WS</th><th>PS</th><th>WS</th><th>PS</th><th>WS</th></tr>
<tr><td>0–22</td><td>1,752</td><td>1,752</td><td colspan="2">Included in 23–64 Age Group</td><td>342</td><td>571</td><td>1,752</td><td>1,752</td><td colspan="2">Included in 23–64 Age Group</td><td>281</td><td>673</td></tr>
<tr><td>23–64</td><td>1,832</td><td>1,832</td><td>537.6[b]</td><td>896[b]</td><td>z</td><td>z</td><td>1,386[a]</td><td>2,198[a]</td><td>430.6[b]</td><td>1,075[b]</td><td>z</td><td>z</td></tr>
<tr><td>over 65</td><td>416</td><td>416</td><td>62.4</td><td>104</td><td>z</td><td>z</td><td>416</td><td>416</td><td>62.4</td><td>104</td><td>z</td><td>z</td></tr>
<tr><td>Total</td><td>4,000</td><td>4,000</td><td>600</td><td>1,000</td><td></td><td></td><td>3,554</td><td>4,366</td><td>493</td><td>1,179</td><td></td><td></td></tr>
</table>

[a] Assume 20 percent of productive people have moved from the poor state to the wealthy state.
[b] These provide essential contrast for last column.
z = Only concerned with 0–22 age group.

investment in education is a long-range investment in the welfare of all citizens of that state. There exists a great difference in the willingness of the various states to support education at the elementary and secondary level as well as higher education. Connecticut, an extremely wealthy state so far as per capita income is concerned, taxes itself for public schools at a very low rate and consequently provides roughly the same expenditure per pupil as does Louisiana, which has a relatively low per capita income, but taxes itself quite heavily for public education. Idaho, with a low per capita income, taxes itself at a very low rate and has a small per pupil expenditure, whereas New York, a very wealthy state in per capita income, taxes itself heavily in order to provide an extremely large amount of money for each pupil in average daily attendance. Texas and Minnesota, during an earlier era, had some people who made wise investments that now provide enormous amounts of money without a burden on taxpayers. If it were decided to provide federal subsidies to improve the quality of the education each child receives, how might this be done in an equitable manner?

EXPENDITURES IN HIGHER EDUCATION

There exists as much variation among the states in expenditures for higher education as for K–12 and the patterns are not predictable on the basis of what is done in K–12. The top five states in the percentage of income spent on higher education in 1971 were Wyoming, South Dakota, North Dakota, Arizona, and New Mexico, while the lowest five states in percentage of per capita income spent on higher education were New Jersey, Massachusetts, Ohio, Connecticut, and New Hampshire. Others near the bottom of the list in per capita expenditures were New York, Pennsylvania, Maryland, and Minnesota. The average expenditure for higher education in the fifty states is 0.785 percent and ranges from Wyoming, which spends 1.49 percent of its income for higher education, to New Jersey, where only 0.31 percent of the per capita income is spent on higher education.

Some state universities, such as the University of Texas at Austin, have gigantic endowments running into hundreds of millions of dollars. The demands on higher education by the citizenry vary greatly from state to state. Wyoming taxes its citizens at a rate nearly five times that of New Jersey. It costs more to educate a student in Boston than it does in Biloxi. How can an equitable formula be worked out to establish equal higher-educational opportunities in this country? The complications of the many variables in financing higher education in the fifty states, as well as political patronage, have thus far stymied equalization of opportunity in higher education as they have in K–12 education. For additional information on this topic, read the report of the Carnegie Commission on Higher Education.[4]

CURRENT STATUS OF EDUCATION FINANCING AND ENROLLMENT

An examination of the data readily reveals the fact that the cost of education is increasing both in absolute terms and in percentage of the gross national product. As shown in Table 1.6, the cost of financing private and public education since 1930 has risen substantially. For the years 1930, 1950, and 1970, respectively, educational financing commanded 3.1 percent, 3.4 percent, and 7.6 percent of the gross national product of the United States.

TABLE 1.6
RISING EDUCATIONAL EXPENDITURES, 1930–70
(In Millions of Dollars)

Educational Level	Years		
	1930	1950	1970
Public Elementary and Secondary Education	2,233	4,869	35,910
Private Elementary and Secondary Education	200	654	4,100
Public Higher Education	237	898	13,400
Private Higher Education	267	808	7,900

SOURCE: *Statistical Abstract of the United States: 1971.*

During the past four decades public higher education has grown much more rapidly than private higher education. In 1930, the majority of the students enrolled in higher education were in private colleges and universities and that sector of the economy utilized more educational dollars than the public sector. By 1970, the picture had changed significantly and both the enrollment and the cost of public higher education were nearly double that of private higher education. Apparently neither sector operates more efficiently overall, since both have increased their per student cost significantly, but at roughly the same rate.

4. *Institutional Aid: Federal Support to Colleges and Universities*, Carnegie Commission on Higher Education (New York: McGraw-Hill Book Co., February 1972).

An overview of the private and public sectors of K–12 education contrasts sharply with an overview of higher education so far as enrollment and expenditures are concerned. While private higher education has lost a very high percentage of the total students enrolled in higher education, K–12 private schools have increased from about 11 percent to nearly 16 percent their percentage of total enrollment. Through 1950, the ratio of expenditures in operational cost per pupil in K–12 education was very similar for the private and the public sectors, but between 1950 and 1970 private education was on the average spending less on each pupil it educated.

Some observers foresee the abolishment of public secondary education if it does not adjust to changing times. A voucher system of education has been advocated by many as one way of creating additional sensitivity to public demands. In several southern states a movement to avoid integrating schools was carried out by creating private schools and then attempting to redirect money that had been a resource of public education.

With larger numbers of people earning upper-middle-class salaries, and the size of families decreasing, a new segment of the population is able to afford private schooling for its offspring. Parents unable to adjust to, or to accept, changing value systems among adolescents, are increasingly turning responsibility for rearing their children to other agencies—among these are private academies. The fact that the labor force is employing a higher percentage of working mothers has increased early-childhood and nursery-school enrollments where both a custodial and an educational function can be combined. The results of such programs generate additional taxpayers whose sympathies for some sort of public support for private education augment those of the segment of the population that historically has supported parochial education by choice and public education by law. The impact of increasing enrollment in private schools may be dampened, however, by two changing patterns in private education. A smaller percentage of the citizenry now makes substantial contributions to churches, and it appears that the youth today are reluctant to enter religious orders and relegate their lives to positions of service without regard for materialistic rewards.

The accumulation of unsatisfied and disillusioned taxpayers has caused a change in the willingness to support public education. Some manifestations of apathy and disgruntlement are the increasing percentage of school-bond proposals that are defeated in elections; an unwillingness to tax for program improvements; an increasing sentiment for federal support of private education, experimental vouchering programs, and educational contracts; and the recent Rodriguez case in the Edgewood schools of San Antonio, which challenged, unsuccessfully, the whole system of local tax support for public education. The greatest change, however, between 1950 and today has been the increase in questioning whether the federal government should support public education to one of openly accepting its money and actively campaigning to increase its financial support of public education.

PUBLIC CONCERNS WITH EDUCATION

Those in positions of educational leadership are seeking ways in which to return public education to the good graces of the consumer. If a businessman finds consumers are not patronizing his marketplace he will endeavor to change or improve his products, services, and prices. A corollary in public education would be to modify it to meet the current demand for relevant education delivered by concerned people at a price the taxpayers are willing to pay.

What are the parameters for these three modifications? A relevant education is one that enables students to become more productive and happier people. It should deal with world problems, such as war, food supply, population, and pollution. It should provide tools for attacking such problems and an attitude of wanting to help solve them. It should not divorce people from their social heritage. It should help them build a healthy self-system, and an economically salable skill. In such a system, parents would be increasingly brought into planning the education, and all concerned parties would be well informed about the objectives of education, the progress a student is making toward achieving his goals, and how their financial contributions are being utilized by the system to support the learning operations. The ledger will probably never be perfectly balanced, but the degree of accountability can certainly become higher than it is today.

Education should be available to the extent that a student is able to profit from it. It should be a life-long opportunity. It should provide the young with useful skills, the productive with marketable vocational information, and the elderly with an opportunity to expand their interests. Its scope can include the development or improvement of verbal skills; the provision of avenues by which interests and aptitudes can be developed; and the improvement and redirection of salable skills. It should enable a person to continually evaluate his niche in the cosmos and to see the implications of the interactions of each person with other people and with nature's endowments. The writers would also advocate that all learners make a meaningful contribution to the support of the kind of education that offers the particular opportunities they seek. With the exception of children, the quality of the education a person receives is probably more affected by the attitude and enthusiasm he displays toward receiving an education than it is by the traditional dispensers of learning. The public can increase the quality of education by rewarding fairly teachers who cause students to want to learn, by refusing to accept unqualified teachers in the schools, and by effectively distributing educational resources in an equitable manner among the population served. A significant area, which has been underexploited to date, is that of informal education. Public support for libraries, educational programs on mass-communication media such as television, thought-provoking columns in newspapers, museums, fine-arts displays, municipal musical organizations, political forums, and scientific displays and information pamphlets might all play a significant part in continuing education, regardless of whether they emanate from a public school, a junior college, a university extension, or some other source. In essence, quality education combines expedient learning with what society deems worthy. Failure to achieve quality education is related to lack of resources and lack of accountability. One approach to improving accountability is the application of economic principles to the problems of education.

ECONOMIC PRINCIPLES RELATED TO EDUCATION

There are more than five hundred different definitions of the term *economics*, ranging from lengthy statements to Jacob Viner's concise "Economics is what economists do." For our purposes in this text, economics is defined as the social science that describes man's efforts to satisfy his material wants by utilizing the scarce resources provided by nature. As a social science, economics involves dealing with human beings, who cannot be controlled as can the physical elements used by the chemists. An economist has society as his laboratory and thus cannot engage in the kind of experimentation favored by the physical scientist. As is true of the social sciences in general, economics is not an exact science and forecasts of economic developments are thus subject to considerable inaccuracies. Economics is, however, the social science with the most sophisticated body of theory; that is, the one with the greatest predictability accuracy of all the social sciences. Our definition underscores the scarcity of resources as an element in the study of any economic activity.

Education is intricately woven into the overall economic process. All societies, explicitly or implicitly, establish economic goals. For example, the goals enumerated below have a high degree of acceptance by most American economists in appraising the American economic system. These economic goals, not necessarily in the order of their importance, are: (1) to provide an increasingly higher living standard for the population; (2) to permit economic freedom; (3) to afford citizens economic security; (4) to produce in accordance with consumer demands; and (5) to distribute income in an equitable manner.

An *increase in living standards* means an increase in the level of real income; that is, an augmented ability of individuals to command goods and services. Money income alone cannot be used as a measure of living standards, for we know that the same sum of money will command different amounts of goods and services at different times. *Economic freedom* is a principle that we, in the United States, have traditionally valued greatly. Economic freedom means the right of the individual to follow his own occupational pursuit unmolested so long as he does not violate existing laws. This type of freedom has never been and can never be a guaranteed reality. *Economic security* is a relative concept. For an upper-middle-class American family, it may mean a continuing income in case of the death of the major bread-winner. However, for a person on the streets of Calcutta, it may merely be a knowledge of where tonight's sleeping quarters will be. There is little doubt that the average man in the United States, or anywhere else, is motivated by the desire for increased economic security. *Production in accordance with consumer demand* means that the consumer is sovereign; his dollar vote determines what will be produced. This concept assumes that the consumer knows what is best for himself. If the consumer is indeed sovereign, then only those producers who cater to his demands will survive; in other words, the real boss is the consumer. *Equitable distribution* of income is a noble goal. Most people abhor the extremes of poverty and wealth that exist in many nations, including our own. We also know that, given a quantity of income, the more equitable distribution is, other things being equal, the greater will be the expenditure for goods and services. For example, ten families with incomes of $10,000 each will usually tend to consume more goods and services than one family with $100,000 of income because there is just so much food, clothing, and shelter that one family can consume.

In attempting to achieve desirable economic goals, perhaps those previously enumerated, what problems are faced by economic societies? Paul Samuelson has stated that certain problems are common to all economies, and to some degree reflect the level of educational priorities. These problems are deciding what to produce, deciding how to produce goods and services, deciding for whom to produce, and deciding what provisions will be made to provide for an expanding economy. These problems must be faced by the primitive African society as well as by the complex United States economy.

Deciding what to produce includes deciding what types of educational services to provide. It is only necessary to read the current literature to know that this is an area of controversy. Frequently, the alternatives are put in terms of guns versus butter. For example, in the United States, the Vietnam War, for a while, resulted in a choice between less consumer goods (butter) so that defense goods (guns) could be produced. The question of how to produce goods is answered differently by different economies. It is resolved by the existing quantities and types of labor, capital, technology, and natural resources. If labor is abundant and capital and technology scarce, we are likely to find a pronounced use of human power relative to machines. This is usually the situation in the underdeveloped economic societies of Asia, Latin America, and Africa, which encompass the major part of the human race. On the other hand, when savings are converted into the capital investment and research that produce technological advances, as has been the case in the United States and Western Europe, society is likely to utilize a smaller proportion of labor relative to capital in its production mix. In such societies labor must have the high level of skill necessary to operate complex capital equipment.

In providing *educational services*, as with the production of any good or service, production possibilities are related to the factors of production. These are land, labor, capital, and enterprise. Education competes with other users of these factors of production in providing services and is subject to the *law of supply and demand* as are other sectors of the economy. This economic principle states that, all other things being equal, prices are determined by the intersection of supply and demand, tending to vary directly with changes in demand and inversely with changes in supply. In other words, the education "industry" must compete for teachers, administrators, and personnel to provide staff-support services. The education industry also competes in the capital market when it has to sell bonds to finance the construction of new buildings. It competes for funds with other users, such as the federal government, business, and private individuals. The same situation exists in regard to building materials, supplies, and utilities. The prices of the services and items needed by educational institutions come under this heading as well. Also, in the marketplace for graduates, the wages, or price, received by graduates of a particular institution are determined to some degree by the market conditions of supply and demand.

Another important economic concept in the educational area is that of *opportunity costs*. By this is meant the cost to an individual in terms of what he is forgoing in the form of earnings by furthering his or her education. A college student, for example, may have an opportunity cost of $8,000 that he could be earning if he were employed rather than attending a university. This concept is also applicable for society as a whole, because when resources are committed to education there is a cost involved in terms of what is given up by these resources not being committed in another sector of the economy. The *cost-benefit principle* is critical in the educational area. This means the dollar amount of benefit derived by the expenditure of a dollar of cost. That is, if society as a whole spends, for example, a billion dollars on education, what benefits are derived from this expenditure? These are somewhat difficult matters to measure. However, with increased sophistication in statistics and the assistance of high-power computers, it is now possible to give some rough approximations in this area.

Historically, society at times markedly increases or decreases its support of education. To some degree, if not totally, this reflects society's view as to the benefits or returns that it is obtaining from educational expenditures. Along these same lines, one of the problems that arises is that of allocating costs among the various levels and types of education. In recent times, for example, there has been a movement towards more support for vocational education. This, to some degree, means that society feels that its return for that particular type of education will be better and a higher amount of expenditures should be committed to it. Another area of difficulty with the cost-benefit approach is deciding who shall derive the benefits. Again, society, by directing its resources to one educational area or another, can to a considerable degree pinpoint the recipients of the benefits of education. In recent times, we have seen a great many programs with financial support intended to assist low-income sectors of our population.

Product differentiation is a fact of life in the business world and this concept is also applicable in education. Educational institutions are engaged in differentiating the services that they provide. In some cases this may take the form of small classes with highly individualized instruction, and in others it might be a very large university with major resources in terms of library, computers, nationally known faculty, and a national image that assists in the placement of graduates. There is also a differentiation among the programs and services offered by the various levels and types of institution, ranging from universities to community colleges, high schools, and trade schools. An effort is made through product differentiation to match the supply of educational services with the demand for these services.

Economies of scale is another economic concept used in education. This means that as an operation is expanded the output increases by a greater amount than the increase in resource commitment. For example, increasing resources by a hundredfold will increase output by more than one hundred. This results from the efficiencies that can be achieved by a large-scale operation. For example, whether an educational institution has a thousand students or twenty thousand, it normally has only one president. This particular administrative cost, if prorated among either the student body or the number of graduates, certainly would result in a smaller per capita cost in the larger institution. Computer facilities are another case in point where a high volume utilization can make per unit use cheaper than can be achieved in a smaller operation. Large-volume buying can result in reduced costs. There is also the problem, however, of diseconomies of scale, which means that the organization has reached a point where an increase of a hundred in resources would result in production increasing by less than one hundred. This occurs when an organization gets so large that it becomes inefficient, bureaucracy sets in, communication channels begin to blur, and the productivity of the work force is reduced.

These basic economic principles have been enumerated simply to point out that education is an industry subject to the same economic principles as any other industry. These concepts may be helpful in understanding the choices that society must make in terms of committing its resources to education or to the many other areas where possible outlets exist. There are differences when education is compared to business in general. The first that comes to mind is the concept of production for profit or for need. Generally, activity in education is undertaken on the basis of need rather than for profit. There are, however, some types of educational activities where the organization is set up as a profit-making entity; in these situations the education industry will more closely approximate the typical business. While economic principles will not give us all the answers, they are generally helpful in obtaining a better understanding of the economic dimensions of our educational system.

BIBLIOGRAPHY

BENSON, CHARLES S. *The Economics of Public Education.* New York: Houghton Mifflin Co., 1968. Not only discusses possible solutions to problems, but provides tables and raw data to afford reader opportunity to develop his own ideas. Chapter entitled "The Federal Role in Financing School Services" opens many avenues of thought. Figure VIII, graph on "Relation Between State Personal Income and Public School Expenditures, 1966," tells at a glance about educational effort in each state; beautiful example of presenting enormous amount of information in minimum of space.

―――. *Perspectives on the Economics of Public Education.* New York: Houghton Mifflin Co., 1963. Excellent source of information on both practical and theoretical solutions to problems of education. Has rare virtue of discussing failures as well as successes. Explains dilemmas that thwart seemingly logical, simple solutions. Easily readable, yet scholarly work, made possible by joint efforts of many well-informed people.

BRAMELD, THEODORE. *The Use of Explosive Ideas in Education.* Pittsburgh: University of Pittsburgh Press, 1965. Makes highly significant point on p. 81: "One important reason good schools develop at all is because good teachers want them to develop—then this sense of dedication to the task of rebuilding is prerequisite to every step of accomplishment."

Carnegie Commission on Higher Education. *Institutional Aid: Federal Support to Colleges and Universities.* New York: McGraw-Hill Book Co., February 1972. Presents many ramifications of financial support for higher education. Contains useful charts and tables. Not comprehensive; e.g., one may find great deal of information about some facet of higher education in Oregon but not for some other state.

KNELLER, GEORGE F. *Foundations of Education.* New York: John Wiley & Sons, 1971. Divided into parts dealing with historical, social, philosophic, scientific, and structural foundations. While Kneller has written in several areas, includes contributions by other authorities. Deals with contemporary issues as well as eternal ones: e.g., readings on education of minorities and about why people should be concerned with death.

PERKES, DAN, and URDANG, LAURENCE, eds. *The Official Associated Press Almanac, 1973.* New York: Almanac Publishing Co., 1972. Has specific sections dealing with facts and figures of education, several other sections dealing indirectly with education. Inexpensive source of current information.

REYNOLDS, JAMES W. *The Comprehensive Junior College Curriculum.* Berkeley: McCutchan Publishing Corp., 1969. Herculean survey of junior college catalogues, synthesized by author with extensive experience and many years as editor of *Junior College Journal*, produces accurate picture of what junior colleges are doing today. Valuable source of data on significance of diverse vocational, technical, and transfer-college programs.

U.S. Department of Commerce, Bureau of the Census. *Statistical Abstract of the United States: 1971.* Washington: U.S. Government Printing Office, 1971. Excellent source of statistical data dealing with many facets of American society.

CHAPTER 2

Economic Contributions of Education

Education makes a very significant contribution to the economy. The purpose of this chapter is to examine the role education plays in the overall economic process. Briefly examined are: (1) productivity and the accompanying factors that govern it, including education; (2) economic growth—its meaning, education and other factors upon which it is based; (3) the impact of education on the world of work; (4) the qualitative aspects of education; and (5) the direct economic impact of education in the United States.

PRODUCTIVITY

Productivity, the output per man-hour, is a critical concept in economic activity. Normally it is impossible for employers to pay workers a wage over a long period of time that exceeds the workers' productivity. Improved living standards of a nation as a whole are generally a result of increases in production, which to varying degrees are governed by the productivity of its labor force. Government policy guidelines, in the battle against inflation, have generally held that wage increases that do not exceed productivity gains are not inflationary, and that those in excess of productivity expansion lead to higher prices. Many controversies in the collective-bargaining area revolve around what share of productivity increases should be allocated to the various factors of production. Productivity is influenced by a variety of factors, such as technology, management, finance, manpower, government, and general economic climate.

Technological factors refer to the ingenuity of engineers and others in devising innovations. These changes are made in the forms of improved tools, equipment, production methods, and types of materials. Most of us are acquainted with the dramatic breakthroughs that have taken place with new machines, assembly-line automation, and the substitution, for example, of plastics for metals. The term *technological revolution* has been used widely and refers to the dramatic pace at which new "know-how" is applied in the economic process. Man now has at his disposal assistance in the form of machines, inanimate power, and new systems procedures that reduce much of his burden and increase his output per hour.

Management factors are critical in the economic production process and refer to the attitudes and behavior of businessmen in carrying out their functions. There are several dimensions to the managerial component. The competitive spirit the manager uses in striving for efficiency has been extremely important in the economy of the United States. Willingness to assume risks and to adopt new innovations are part of this factor. Efficient scheduling of work, including division of labor and plant layout in striving for worker productivity, is generally a managerial function. Judicious purchasing of materials, in terms of quality, cost, and timely delivery scheduling, are important production dimensions. The drive for expansion of markets is made possible by higher-volume production and in many cases results in accompanying reduced costs. Efficient handling of labor relations can lead to a morale situation where the worker will strive to produce more and thus increase his productivity. The support of research and development programs seeking new and better production methods is important. Finally, the standardization of products and the accompanying use of interchangeable parts has made possible mass production with increased output per hour and reduced costs.

Financial considerations are important in understanding productivity. The availability of funds for financing new innovations, as well as expansion to realize economies of scale, plays an important part in productivity. This may be viewed as taking place both in existing industries and in starting new types of enterprises. If the investment is to be made, financial capital must be available at a cost that does not exceed the expected net rate of return on the undertaking. In a nation like the United States, capital funds have been available because in recent times, in any given year, our nation has invested approximately 18 percent of its gross national product. However, this problem may be acute in underdeveloped countries where savings are low because productivity is low. In such cases either the needed capital improvements are not made or these countries must rely on external sources of assistance to make investment possible.

The labor factor is a critical determinant of productivity. The degree of skill the labor force possesses is obtained through one form or another of the educational process. Increases in the level and range of labor-force skills may be viewed by society as investment in human capital. Accompanying the skills is the matter of the general education of workers and how to impress on them their role in the production process. The health of the labor force is not a major factor in the United States, but it can be in a country like India, where malnutrition and uncontrolled diseases take their toll in loss of strength and a high incidence of sickness. Morale is critical and is a function of labor and managerial activity as related to labor relations. Education again may play a part because if the worker understands his role well, he is likely to be a more productive individual. The hours that the labor force works are a major determinant of how much is produced and the adaptability of this group is a major factor in productivity. With a changing economy it is important that workers be able to adapt to new working conditions and demands imposed by technological changes. Geographical mobility helps the productivity factor for the nation as a whole. A mobile labor force will move into areas where demand for workers is high and leave surplus-labor areas, thereby making a greater contribution to national output, and this normally results in more output per hour because the mobile worker can supply his skills where they are needed. The willingness of workers to accept innovations is important, as are their attitudes toward "featherbedding" or make-work situations. In situations where "featherbedding" exists, such as the railroad industry, it tends to reduce output per man-hour. Compensation incentives may stimulate a worker's performance and in some industries financial payments based totally or in part on performance have increased production.

Governmental factors, that is, governmental policies as they relate to the various areas of business activity, play a prominent role in productivity. Competition, which is a regulating force in our type of economic structure, has seen involvement of the government sector. There are several notable examples of governmental effort to promote competition. The *Interstate Commerce Commission*, created in 1887, forbade the railroads the right to grant special rates, secret rebates, or drawbacks. Discrimination between persons, places, and commodities in rate-making was prohibited, and under some conditions it became illegal to charge more for a short haul than a long haul. Railroads were not allowed to form pooling agreements, or to deny the public the right to inspect schedules and rates. The *Sherman Act of 1890* declared illegal every contract, combination, or conspiracy in restraint of trade or commerce among the several states, or with sovereign nations.

The *Clayton Antitrust Act of 1914* was a punitive piece of legislation. It has many provisions, but basically it (1) listed unlawful methods of business competition; (2) prohibited interlocking directorships in certain banking institutions and in organizations engaged in interstate commerce; (3) indicated ways of obtaining relief from illegal trade practices; and (4) exempted labor unions from the antitrust provisions of the Sherman Antitrust Act. Sometimes the very size of a business presents problems in the view of the government. Such was the case with the Alcoa Company of America, which in 1945 was told to divest itself of some of its interests simply because of its size. No malpractices were found in the Alcoa operation and after the court order was put into effect, Alcoa had to raise the price of aluminum in order not to drive its newly government-created competitors out of business.[1]

Taxation is a government power that affects productivity in a variety of ways. For example, depreciation policies can reduce replacement of worn-out and obsolete equipment. Subsidies of various types can also be a major factor; for example, the government may subsidize retraining programs to help individuals acquire new skills. Tariffs, a government tax on imports, can permit mass production of goods that might otherwise be supplied by other countries. Tariffs tend to keep out foreign competition and thus may permit greater production at home at a volume where economies of scale are realized, with efficiencies resulting in augmented productivity. In recent times the governmental attitude toward business, whether friendly or hostile, has brought about changes that have led to productivity improvement.

Other *general economic factors* have a bearing on productivity. Examples of these are the willingness of individuals to accept new products and thus warrant risk-taking action on the part of the innovative producer. The willingness of the public to save and invest influences the availability of funds and the cost of these funds for capital improvements or additions. Public investment in transportation influences the degree to which specialization can be practiced. Excellent transportation facilities lead to greater division of labor and resources on a geographical basis. Inadequate transportation leads to more self sufficiency and, perhaps, reduced productivity.

The earning power of individuals is related to productivity and to the supply and demand of the particular service under consideration. As stated previously, output per man-hour, or whatever other time unit is used, tends to set a ceiling on employee compensation once the output is converted into dollars and cents. An increase in demand for the services of individuals, other things being equal, tends to lead to higher payments in the form of wages paid to the individuals. When the supply of a particular skill is increasing faster than the demand for that skill, it generally results in reduced wages and salary payments. Organized labor plays a role in

1. Ross M. Robertson, *History of the American Economy*, 2d ed. (New York: Harcourt, Brace & World, 1964), p. 567.

controlling the supply of labor, and unions endeavor to pursue policies that will result in wages being higher than they would be in the absence of unions. Basically, unions make possible a collective-bargaining situation in which the combined power of the labor force in an organization or industry meets with an employer or several employers. This tends to equalize the bargaining process, as compared to what it might be if each individual worker had to bargain separately. There appears to be a significant relationship between the educational level and the earning power of individuals. In 1969 males twenty-five years old and over, with at least four years of college, earned on the average during a lifetime $586,000; those with a high school diploma earned $350,000; and persons who had completed eight years of elementary school, $258,000. The annual mean income for an individual with under eight years of elementary schooling was $3,981, as compared to $12,938 for a person with four more years of college.[2]

In the area of productivity, education functions to improve the quality of human effort, thereby generally enabling society to realize increased output per man-hour. As Theodore W. Schultz has stated: "Measured by what labor contributes to output, the productive capacity of human beings is now vastly larger than all other forms of wealth taken together."[3] Some find it distasteful to look upon a human being as capital because traditionally we have not viewed individuals as capital, except if they were slaves. In fact, much of man's evolution has been a struggle to eradicate systems of indentured servitude thereby allowing individuals more freedom. Today it is evident that the human component in the productive process is becoming increasingly important. Profitable innovation is becoming more difficult to achieve because the easiest and most productive applications of capital have already been made. Given the current state of technology, many of our formerly excellent natural resources have been depleted. Furthermore, expansion in the size of organizations has led to situations where operations are encountering diseconomies of scale. These factors point to the increasing importance of developing the human component in the production process. Knowledge and skills do have economic value and are indispensable to a society attempting to achieve high levels of efficient economic activity.

Table 2.1 presents data on the relationship between productivity, compensation, and unit-labor costs in the United States for selected years from 1950 to 1970. Several observations can be made from the data in this

---

2. *Statistical Abstract of the United States: 1971*, p. 111.
3. Theodore W. Schultz, "Investment in Human Capital," *American Economic Review* 51, no. 1 (March 1961):2.

TABLE 2.1
Output Per Man-Hour, Hourly Compensation, and Unit-Labor Costs in the Private Economy, 1950-70

Item	1950	1955	1960	1965	1968	1969	1970
Output,[a] total private	52.5	64.3	71.9	91.8	104.9	107.9	107.4
Nonfarm industries, total	51.3	63.4	71.1	91.5	105.1	108.3	107.9
Manufacturing	51.3	65.0	68.6	92.7	106.7	110.9	106.4
Nonmanufacturing	51.4	62.5	72.5	90.9	104.3	106.9	108.7
Man-Hours,[b] total private	87.9	92.1	92.0	97.4	101.9	104.1	102.7
Nonfarm industries, total	79.0	86.1	88.6	96.3	102.1	104.9	103.9
Manufacturing	79.8	88.2	85.8	94.3	101.9	103.7	98.5
Nonmanufacturing	78.6	85.2	89.9	97.2	102.3	105.5	106.5
Output per man-hour, total private	59.7	69.9	78.2	94.2	102.9	103.7	104.6
Nonfarm industries, total	65.0	73.6	80.3	95.1	102.9	103.2	103.8
Manufacturing	64.4	73.7	79.9	98.3	104.7	106.9	108.1
Nonmanufacturing	65.3	73.4	80.6	93.5	101.9	101.4	102.1
Compensation per man-hour,[c] total private	42.8	55.9	71.7	88.4	107.6	115.4	123.6
Nonfarm industries, total	45.3	58.6	73.9	89.2	107.3	114.5	122.3
Manufacturing	44.7	60.0	76.6	91.2	107.1	113.9	121.6
Nonmanufacturing	45.7	57.6	72.6	88.3	107.5	115.0	123.3
Unit-labor cost, total private	71.7	80.1	91.8	93.8	104.6	111.3	118.2
Nonfarm industries, total	69.7	79.6	92.0	93.9	104.3	111.0	117.8
Manufacturing	69.5	81.4	95.9	92.8	102.3	106.6	112.5
Nonmanufacturing	69.9	78.4	90.0	94.4	105.4	113.5	120.8

[a] Refers to gross national product in 1958 prices.
[b] Hours of all persons in private industry engaged in production, includes man-hours of proprietors and unpaid family workers. Based primarily on establishment data.
[c] Wages and salaries of employees plus employers' contribution for social insurance and private benefit plans. Also includes an estimate of wages, salaries, and supplemental payments for the self-employed.

SOURCE: *Economic Report of the President*, February 1971. Data from U.S. Department of Labor, Bureau of Labor Statistics.

table. Between 1960 and 1970 output per man-hour in the private sector of the economy increased by 26.4 index points. However, compensation per man-hour during the same time period rose by 51.9 index points. As a result of this situation there was an increase of 26.4 index points in the per-unit labor costs, which placed considerable inflationary pressures on the economy. That is, workers received compensation increments in excess of the increases in their output per man-hour and the differential had to be covered either by reductions in profits or by increases in prices. In a free-enterprise democratic society like the United States, this kind of situation frequently results in higher prices. One of the best ways to combat inflation is through increments in productivity. Education abets this process when it helps make possible new technological breakthroughs, provides advances in systems designs, and results in providing a highly trained labor force.

ECONOMIC GROWTH AND EDUCATION

Productivity is one of the components in economic growth that enhances economic activity through greater efficiency in the use of resources. For our purposes, *economic growth* is considered to be an increase in real gross national product; that is, the increase in output measured in terms of current prices has been adjusted for price changes. Economic growth is important because it results in an expansion of the gross national product, which is the sum of goods and services available to consumers.

What factors are responsible for economic growth? The answer to this complex question must be treated here in a summary fashion. Much remains to be learned by economists and other social scientists regarding the relative importance of the various economic growth factors. *The major elements in the economic growth process are usually considered to be: (1) population, (2) natural resources, (3) capital, (4) education and technology, (5) entrepreneur and (6) government, not necessarily in this order of importance.*

Population, from which the labor force is obtained, is one of the four factors of production, the others being land, capital, and the entrepreneur. The role of population in the economic growth process is varied. The size of the population is critical. India and China, for example, would probably be better off economically with smaller populations. On the other hand, Australia and Canada might benefit from a larger number of inhabitants. In the latter two cases, larger population might lead to larger domestic markets and increased utilization of the vast natural resources that are present in these two large land areas. The rate at which the number of people is expanding is also significant and in economically backward countries rapidly expanding populations tend to further reduce living standards, or to make improvements in living conditions difficult to achieve. The skills that the population possesses are critical and in some regions, such as India, there are large numbers of individuals with very low skill-levels. This type of population is not an asset, but a liability in an era which is experiencing a decline in the need for unskilled laborers and an increasing demand for skilled workers of various kinds. The labor-force participation rate is an indication of how much of the total population is contributing to economic production.

Expanding population is putting pressures on the world's known resources. In the case of land, for example, there are about 196,836,000 square miles of earth surface and only 57,168,000 square miles, or about 33 percent, are cultivatable. In addition to arable land, natural resources include climate, water, minerals, forests, habor facilities, and navigable waterways. Resources aid economic progress only if they are utilized. Some nations with excellent resource bases, such as the Congo and Brazil, have low living standards, while others, such as Switzerland and England, have high living standards despite relatively inferior natural resources.

As we have already indicated, *capital*, which refers to man-made goods, such as machines, tools, and factory buildings that are used in further production, is important in productivity gains and also in economic growth. Capital accumulation is one of the factors that distinguishes the advanced nations from the underdeveloped ones. The use of capital helps increase a nation's output of economic goods because accelerated utilization of capital generally means larger-scale production, more specialization, and greater efficiency. Increasing capital accumulation is necessary if the labor force is expanded. How do nations accumulate capital? Countries, like people, must save part of their production and they cannot consume all that they produce. This presents problems to the poor nations because their levels of production and living standards are low.

The *entrepreneur* is the individual who puts land, labor, and capital together. Originally, he was a risk-taker in the sense that he was the investor of capital as well as the manager of the firm. Examples of this type are Henry Ford, J. Pierpont Morgan, and Andrew Carnegie. Today we have a highly skilled labor-managerial group, which combines the factors of production. The managers are entrepreneurs in that they are investors in the firms they manage and thus assume risks; however, today many have only limited stock holdings in their firms and their role as entrepreneurs is reduced.

The role of the *government* is important in the economic development process. In the United States our economic system is generally regarded as one of free enterprise built by private ownership of the factors of production with little governmental participation. However, the government has played a great role in economic progress. In the transportation area, for example, after unsuccessful initial efforts to provide roads on a private enterprise basis, it became clear that this was a job to be done collectively. The railroads developed with considerable assistance from the government, particularly in the form of land grants, and state governments have traditionally played an important role in providing power facilities. Thus, "social overhead capital" in our nation traditionally has been to a great degree supplied through public activity.

Education is an important factor in economic growth. When society spends funds for schools, libraries, and teachers to educate its youth, it is investing in human capital, which may be the most important factor of economic growth. Education widens the individual's horizon so that he becomes more cognizant of local economic opportunities, providing more pervasive knowledge of economic opportunities, which enhances the efficient utilization of available resources. Managerial ability is the most important factor governing the productivity of labor, given a set of capital facilities and natural resources. Our reference to widening horizons is ably substantiated by the statement of Walter Krause, an Iowa University economist, that "education is useful as one part of a program of development in that it can enhance the productive capacities of the population, can help spark imagination and spur incentive, and can help dissolve impediments associated with cultural rigidity."[4]

In a society in which a chief characteristic is change, higher educational attainment gives the individual greater flexibility in adapting to new demands. In reference to this point, Charles P. Kindleberger, Massachusetts Institute of Technology economist, writes that "education sends out its effects in many directions. The spread of calculation is basic to income maximization. Capacity to communicate is needed for organized markets with formal prices. A minimum of rationality and understanding of cause and effect are prerequisites for changes in techniques."[5]

The Committee for Economic Development (CED), which is composed of leading American scholars on economic growth, feels that "the greatest economic source of any nation is its people. Satisfying economic growth requires that the people be educated, mobile, and motivated to seek improvement of their lives."[6] In a study analyzing the forces responsible

---

4. Walter Krause, *Economic Development: The Underdeveloped World and the American Interest* (San Francisco: Wadsworth Publishing Co., 1961), p. 87.

5. Charles P. Kindleberger, *Economic Development* (New York: McGraw-Hill, 1958), p. 313.

6. *Cooperation for Progress in Latin America* (Washington: Committee for Economic Development, 1961), p. 17.

for the remarkable economic growth in the United States, CED commented that the diffusion of education throughout the entire population was of extreme importance. Specifically, CED stated that:

... the kinds of skills called for in our modern technological society are multitudinous. Widespread education has provided the necessary basic groundwork both for the acquisition of such skills and for adaptation to changing requirements. Also, education weakens the force of outmoded custom and tradition. Consequently, changes in working conditions and methods are welcomed, rather than resisted, among American working people and their leaders more often than among those of many countries. Still further, the diffusion of education has an immense influence, in diverse ways, in making consumers receptive to new goods and services. All this, of course, is quite aside from the vital non-economic values of education.[7]

Economically advanced nations are usually characterized by rapid *technological changes* and educational systems that stress science and technologically oriented subjects. Desirable technological change requires forward-looking businessmen, government officials, and agrarian leaders, who are not committed to perpetuation of past patterns but are willing to try something new if it holds the promise of being better than what they are already using. Technological change presupposes that some equipment and human skills will become obsolete before they are depreciated. Thus, one is likely to find that the old saying, "There are two certain things in the world, change and resistance to change," is to a great degree applicable to this factor of economic development. Workers are particularly apprehensive about losing their jobs to machines. This is not a new development; in the days of the Industrial Revolution, workers returned at night when plants were closed and smashed machines which they viewed as a threat to their earning of a livelihood. Thus, in addition to having the technological know-how, a society must be geared to accept change. We note that in the post–World War II period, even when capital and accompanying new technology were introduced in some underdeveloped regions, there was resistance to changing tradition-bound methods of doing things.

It should be noted that technological progress is not without a price. Human skills and existing machines are often rendered obsolete and the cost of carrying on the research that leads to new developments is high. It may well be that the major contribution the Western nations are making to the economic development process of the underdeveloped regions of the world is that of sending them technological know-how. Much

---

7. *Economic Growth in the United States, Its Past and Future* (Washington: Committee for Economic Development, 1961), p. 24.

of this know-how goes free to these regions and without prior investment in research they reap the benefits obtained in the advanced nations. Equipment purchased can be reproduced; information in technical literature can be utilized; scientists and technicians from the advanced nations, who are sent to the underdeveloped regions, impart their knowledge and the benefits of their research to the local people.

In summary, *it is apparent that education and technology are important in the economic process and that skills are a part of human capital; furthermore, skills are normally obtained through one form or another of education.* Some economists, such as Theodore Schultz, believe that the differences in the skill-levels of populations are probably the major factor causing differences in economic growth-rates among various countries. With the proper education of the population, natural-resource utilization tends to be enhanced and outmoded customs and traditions to be weakened. Capacity to communicate is improved and new industries are attracted by skilled labor groups and enlightened consumers. Furthermore, an enlightened citizenry with a high civic awareness can provide a climate that is attractive for industrial location.

AREAS OF INVESTMENT

What forms can investment in human capital take? There is the traditional education formally organized at the elementary, secondary, and higher levels. A variety of programs may be pursued by students, presumably following major areas of interest, and hopefully this reflects where their abilities are the strongest. A very fundamental question with regard to formal education is: What should be its mission? That is, should education be geared to providing skills that are readily usable in the economy, or should it provide well-rounded backgrounds for individuals to enable them to lead richer lives? Our system has provided alternatives for individuals with different interests and capabilities. Nevertheless, it is apparent that educational institutions have not always kept abreast of labor-force skill needs, and while the training provided may be sound, it sometimes provides individuals with outmoded skills. The current trend, in the early part of the 1970s, appears to be toward more vocational education at all levels. This has partly resulted from the spectacle of college students not being able to find employment in the fields in which they have been trained.

The *health* of the population, and in particular of the labor force, is another form of investment. Health expenditures include all activities that have an influence on the life expectancy, strength, and stamina of the population. Health training can also be a part of the education process and in some areas even rudimentary training in sanitation and diet would be extremely helpful. In the United States, one current form of health education is emphasizing to our population the need to exercise for physical well-being. In a formal, organized school setting, education for health is assuming new importance in preparing individuals to function and to survive in an economic setting that generally requires more mental than physical efforts.

On-the-job training reported by government and industry is a new way of trying to overcome human obsolescence. There are many programs in this area, activated by the basic tenet that individual skills have not kept pace with technological change and that human resources need to be upgraded. Individuals earn while they learn in most of these programs, which makes the educational retraining process less painful. One of the questions with this type of education is: Who pays? That is, should retraining be a burden on the business sector, or does society have a responsibility to subsidize totally or in part the combating of human obsolescence? Joint ventures of business and government seem to have some value. The business firm normally has available space and equipment and generally needs the skills that are being taught to individuals. The government, on the other hand, through subsidization, perhaps in the form of wages during the training process, still saves if the business firms provide training facilities.

Adult education programs are geared to providing skills for individuals who are employed but see the need for upgrading. This type of program is offered across the board by various educational institutions. Even labor unions have educational programs of this type, which enable members to enhance their level of knowledge and skills. Given the very rapid changes in technological know-how, it appears that this kind of educational undertaking will increase in the future.

With the rapid changes in our economic structure, it is imperative that individuals be mobile enough to move to where their skills are needed and away from where they are in over-supply. Again, it is apparent that education helps in making individuals more mobile, and to the extent that this is achieved the economy benefits.

Unemployment, underemployment, and human obsolescence are major problems facing a rapidly advancing technological society. The productive potential of an unemployed person, when not used, is lost forever; this represents a drain on the total economy, because individuals who are not producers are still consumers. Table 2.2 presents data on the labor force, employment, and unemployment in the United States during 1950-72 for

TABLE 2.2

Population, Labor Force, Employment, and Unemployment, 1950-72

Year	Total Non-institutional Population	Total including Armed Forces	Labor Force — Civilian Labor Force Total	Percent of Population	Employed Total	Agri-cultural	Non-agri-cultural	Unemployed Number	Unemployed Percent	Not in Labor Force Total[a]	Keeping House[b]	In School[b]
1950	106,645	63,858	62,208	58.3	58,920	7,160	51,760	3,288	5.3	42,787	33,058	6,197
1955	112,732	68,072	65,023	57.7	62,171	6,449	55,724	2,852	4.4	44,660	33,722	6,569
1960	119,759	72,142	69,628	58.1	65,778	5,458	60,318	3,852	5.5	47,617	34,543	8,162
1964	127,224	75,830	73,091	57.5	69,305	4,523	64,782	3,786	5.2	51,394	35,454	10,510
1965	129,236	77,178	74,455	57.6	71,088	4,361	66,726	3,366	4.5	52,058	35,556	11,094
1966	131,180	78,893	75,770	57.8	72,895	3,979	68,915	2,875	3.8	52,288	35,316	11,148
1967	133,320	80,793	77,347	58.0	74,372	3,844	70,528	2,975	3.8	52,527	34,993	6,657
1968	135,562	82,272	78,737	58.1	75,920	3,817	72,103	2,817	3.6	53,291	35,204	6,900
1969	137,841	84,239	80,733	58.6	77,902	3,606	74,296	2,831	3.5	53,602	34,888	7,013
1970	140,182	85,903	82,715	59.0	78,627	3,462	75,165	4,088	4.9	54,280	35,118	7,033
1971	142,596	85,929	84,173	59.0	79,120	3,387	75,732	4,993	5.9	55,666	35,361	7,523
1972, Apr.	145,229	87,787	85,324	58.8	80,627	3,287	77,339	4,697	5.5	57,442	35,622	9,396

[a] Includes "other," not shown separately.
[b] 1950-66, persons fourteen years old and over.
SOURCE: *Statistical Abstract of the United States: 1972*, p. 216.

persons sixteen years of age and over. As can be noted from the data, the highest unemployment rate was experienced in 1971, with 5.7 percent of the civilian labor force out of work, while the lowest occurred in 1969, when only 3.5 percent of the labor pool was seeking work yet unable to find employment.

Table 2.3 presents unemployment percentages for selected years from 1955 to 1972 by category of worker. The data cover persons sixteen years of age and over, and prior to 1960 Alaska and Hawaii are excluded. These data reveal that unemployment is generally lowest among white married men, and is highest among black women. The ratio of unemployment of black and other minority races to white was 1:8. Looking at these data, *it would appear that those who generally have a higher level of educational attainment experience the least amount of unemployment.*

One of the difficulties encountered with education in the economic process is the possible *underinvestment in minority groups.* Table 2.4 presents the number of years of school completed in the United States by race and age as of 1970. The data cover individuals fourteen years of age and over. It is apparent that educational achievement is much lower among blacks than among all races combined. The data are particularly telling in the category of completion of four years of college or more, where 9.1 percent of all races attained this level and only 3.5 percent of blacks. Also, 25.7 percent of the blacks have less than seven years of formal schooling. This means that a sector of the population is probably not adequately trained for the needs of the economy, and some way to compensate for this may have to be subsidized with some form of welfare expenditure.

Table 2.5 presents high school graduates and school dropouts sixteen to twenty-one years of age for selected years between 1965 and 1970. While 11.6 percent of high school graduates were unemployed in 1970, the figure was 21.5 percent for dropouts. During the same year, 78.4 percent of the graduates were in the labor force, compared to 58.4 percent of the dropout group. The picture is quite clear that lack of completion of school results in a much larger percentage of the total group not being in the labor force. Once again the data indicate that the black and other minority groups have a much higher percentage of illiteracy than does the white population.

Table 2.6, offering data for 1959 and 1970, presents major occupational groups of employed persons by sex, race, and years of school completed. In 1959, 65.4 percent of the blue-collar workers, compared to 5.3 percent of the white-collar workers, had less than four years of high school. Corresponding percentages for 1970 were 71.6 and 8.8 respectively.

It would be oversimplifying the matter if education were portrayed as a cure-all and as the savior from all problems that befall our economy.

TABLE 2.3
Percentage of Labor Force Unemployed, 1955–72

Subject	1955	1960	1965	1967	1968	1969	1970	1971	April 1972
Total, unemployed (in thousands)	2,852	3,852	3,366	2,975	2,817	2,831	4,088	4,993	4,697
Labor-force time lost[a] (percentage)	4.8	6.7	5.0	4.2	4.0	3.9	5.4	6.4	5.8
Unemployment rate (percentage)[b]									
All workers	4.4	5.5	4.5	3.8	3.6	3.5	4.9	5.9	5.5
White	3.9	4.9	4.1	3.4	3.2	3.1	4.5	5.4	5.1
Male	3.7	4.8	3.6	2.7	2.6	2.5	4.0	4.9	4.7
Female	4.3	5.3	5.0	4.6	4.3	4.2	5.4	6.3	5.7
Black and other	8.7	10.2	8.1	7.4	6.7	6.4	8.2	9.9	9.0
Male	8.8	10.7	7.4	6.0	5.6	5.3	7.3	9.1	8.4
Female	8.4	9.4	9.2	9.1	8.3	7.8	9.3	10.8	9.6
Ratio, black and other to white	2.2	2.1	2.0	2.2	2.1	2.1	1.8	1.8	1.8
Blue-collar workers	NA	NA	NA	4.4	4.1	3.9	6.2	6.7	6.9
White-collar workers	NA	NA	NA	2.2	2.0	2.1	2.8	2.6	3.0
Experienced wage and salary workers	NA	NA	NA	3.6	3.4	3.3	4.8	5.7	5.1
Married men, wife present	NA	NA	NA	1.8	1.6	1.5	2.6	3.2	3.0
White	NA	NA	NA	1.7	1.5	1.4	2.4	3.0	2.8
Black and other	NA	NA	NA	3.2	2.9	2.5	3.9	5.0	4.4

[a] Man-hours lost by the unemployed and persons on part-time for economic reasons as a percent of potentially available labor force man-hours.
[b] Percent of civilian labor force in specified group.
NA = Data not available.
SOURCE: *Statistical Abstract of the United States: 1972*, p. 221.

TABLE 2.4
Years of School Completed, by Race and Age, 1970

Race and Age	Population (1,000)	Elementary School 0–4 years	Elementary School 5–7 years	Elementary School 8 years	High School 1–3 years	High School 4 years	College 1–3 years	College 4 years or more	Median School Years Completed
All races	147,472	4.1	8.7	13.1	21.7	32.0	11.2	9.1	12.1
14–17 years	15,669	0.9	15.4	26.3	56.5	0.8	0.1	—	9.3
18 and 19 years	6,901	0.7	1.7	2.4	34.2	47.8	13.2	—	12.2
20–24 years	15,593	0.9	2.1	2.9	13.6	43.0	28.7	8.8	12.7
25 years and over	109,310	5.3	9.1	13.4	17.1	34.0	10.2	11.0	12.2
25–29 years	13,513	1.1	2.5	4.2	16.8	44.1	14.9	16.4	12.6
30–34 years	11,352	1.6	4.0	5.1	17.5	43.8	13.0	15.1	12.5
35–44 years	23,021	2.7	6.1	8.4	18.5	40.5	11.0	12.8	12.4
45–54 years	23,298	3.6	7.7	12.0	18.4	38.1	10.1	10.0	12.2
55 years and over	38,126	10.4	15.5	22.9	15.4	21.0	7.3	7.5	9.3
Black	14,828	10.7	15.2	12.3	28.2	23.3	6.8	3.5	10.2
14–17 years	2,025	1.4	23.0	28.4	46.1	1.1	0.1	—	8.9
18 and 19 years	887	1.1	3.7	4.8	48.8	33.9	7.6	—	11.7
20–24 years	1,826	1.6	3.8	3.9	25.7	42.4	19.3	3.3	12.4
25 years and over	10,089	15.1	16.7	11.2	23.3	23.4	5.9	4.5	9.9
25–29 years	1,453	2.5	4.7	5.6	31.1	39.0	9.8	7.3	12.2
30–34 years	1,198	3.3	9.8	4.6	32.3	37.6	7.8	4.6	12.0
35–44 years	2,347	7.1	12.7	10.9	27.8	29.4	7.0	5.2	11.2
45–54 years	2,128	12.4	20.0	15.2	23.3	19.8	5.5	3.8	9.3
55 years and over	2,962	34.2	26.3	13.9	12.5	7.7	2.5	2.9	6.2

SOURCE: U.S. Department of Commerce, *Current Population Reports*, Series P-20, No. 207.

TABLE 2.5

Employment Status of High School Graduates and School Dropouts, 1965–70

Employment Status, Sex, and Race	Graduates					Dropouts			
	1965	1968	1969	1970	1965	1968	1969	1970
Civilian noninstitutional population	4,898	5,418	5,339	5,823	2,986	2,734	2,683	2,757
Not in labor force	1,129	1,342	1,115	1,247	1,123	1,071	1,096	1,146
In labor force	3,769	4,076	4,223	4,566	1,863	1,663	1,588	1,611
Percent of population	76.9	75.2	79.1	78.4	62.4	60.8	59.2	58.4
Male	1,617	1,513	1,650	1,966	1,265	1,041	977	1,024
Female	2,152	2,563	2,573	2,600	598	622	611	587
White	3,375	3,598	3,742	4,065	1,469	1,315	1,223	1,243
Black and other	394	478	481	501	394	348	365	368
Employed	3,451	3,760	3,897	4,038	1,585	1,415	1,358	1,264
Percent of labor force	91.6	92.2	92.3	88.4	85.1	85.1	85.5	78.5
Male	1,512	1,419	1,540	1,730	1,105	913	808	805
Female	1,939	2,341	2,357	2,308	480	502	490	459
White	3,116	3,344	3,490	3,636	1,266	1,153	1,058	1,011
Black and other	335	416	406	402	319	262	301	253
Unemployed	318	316	326	528	278	248	230	347
Percent of labor force	8.4	7.8	7.7	11.6	14.9	14.9	14.5	21.5
Male	105	94	110	236	160	128	109	219
Female	213	222	216	292	118	120	121	128
White	259	254	250	429	203	162	165	232
Black and other	59	62	76	99	75	86	65	115

Source: U.S. Department of Labor, *Special Labor Force Report*, Nos. 66, 108, 121, and forthcoming report.

TABLE 2.6
OCCUPATIONS AND EDUCATIONAL LEVELS OF EMPLOYED PERSONS, 1959 AND 1970

Year, Sex, and Occupation Group	WHITE Total	WHITE Less than 4 Years of High School	WHITE 4 Years of High School or More	BLACK AND OTHER Total	BLACK AND OTHER Less than 4 Years of High School	BLACK AND OTHER 4 Years of High School or More
1959						
Male, number (in thousands)	37,766	18,740	19,026	3,744	2,928	816
Percent by occupation:						
White-collar	39.7	20.3	58.8	12.6	5.3	38.8
Blue-collar	45.5	58.9	32.3	59.3	65.4	37.3
Service, incl. private household workers	5.6	7.2	4.0	14.3	12.6	20.2
Farm	9.2	13.7	4.9	13.9	16.7	3.7
Female, number (in thousands)	17,776	6,994	10,782	2,484	1,725	759
Percent by occupation:						
White-collar	61.1	31.5	80.3	17.6	5.8	44.5
Blue-collar	17.2	31.4	8.0	14.7	15.7	12.4
Service, incl. private household workers	18.5	31.6	10.0	64.3	73.8	42.6
Farm	3.2	5.5	1.6	3.4	4.7	0.5
1970						
Male, number (in thousands)	42,434	14,701	27,733	4,629	2,626	2,003
Percent by occupation						
White-collar	44.3	18.5	58.0	23.2	8.8	42.1
Blue-collar	45.0	64.8	34.6	61.1	71.6	47.3
Service, incl. private household workers	5.6	7.5	4.6	11.1	12.6	9.2
Farm	5.0	9.1	2.9	4.6	7.0	1.4
Female, number (in thousands)	25,040	6,926	18,114	3,551	1,656	1,895
Percent by occupation						
White-collar	64.7	30.3	77.9	35.1	10.3	56.8
Blue-collar	16.3	35.6	9.0	18.4	21.5	15.8
Service, incl. private household workers	17.5	31.0	12.3	45.8	67.0	27.3
Farm	1.5	3.2	0.8	0.7	1.2	0.2

SOURCE: U.S. Department of Labor, *Special Labor Force Report, No. 125.*

At times there has been *overinvestment* in some forms of education, particularly at the higher level. The result is the production of college graduates who do not have marketable skills, and either find themselves unemployed or are forced to accept jobs that require less know-how than they possess, consequently becoming frustrated and unhappy individuals. There is an urgent need, from an economic point of view, to bring about the proper balance of supply and demand of labor-force skills. This is an extremely difficult goal, particularly in a free-enterprise economy that is not subject to direct governmental controls. The market arena becomes the scene where the decision-making process takes place in the form of prices paid for labor of various kinds and the amount of services demanded and supplied.

We have already discussed the indirect role of education in the economic process. *Education as an industry making direct expenditures is truly a major economic factor in the United States.* In 1970 there were 59,261,000 students enrolled during the daytime at all levels of education. Of this number, 37,133,000 were in elementary schools, 14,715,000 in high schools, and 7,413,000 in colleges and universities. Overall, there was a 52.8 percent increase in total school enrollment during the decade of the 1950s and a 28.1 percent increment during the decade of the 1960s. During 1971, expenditures both public and private, by all types of institution, amounted to $75.3 billion, or approximately 7.7 percent of the gross national product. In 1970, there were approximately 3,100,000 teachers employed in the United States at all levels of education. Data are unavailable as to the number of supporting staff employed by the education industry. Thus, in addition to the very critical and more important indirect contributions of education to the economic process, education itself is a very significant part of daily economic activity in the United States.[8]

SUMMARY

In summary, the role of education in economic activity becomes clear. Economic growth is to a great degree dependent on productivity, which in turn is dependent upon technological and human know-how, which in turn rely on education. The human component is the most important factor in the overall economic development effort, and those with a high degree of skills contribute more to efficiency and total output. High-production individuals are usually well compensated by society for their services, which is reflected in higher incomes and a reduced rate of unemploy-

---

8. *Statistical Abstract of the United States: 1971*, p. 111.

ment for this group. Given a modern, advanced technological society and its accompanying great degree of change, education assists by giving the individual more flexibility to adapt to new situations. The matter is not a simple one, however, and there is a danger of overinvestment and an oversupply of individuals relative to the demand for a particular type of skill. On the other hand, it is evident that there has been a considerable amount of underinvestment in minority groups, which has led to the underdevelopment of this resource in the economic growth process of the United States. Expenditures on education are an important direct contribution to the American economy.

BIBLIOGRAPHY

BRANDIS, ROYALL. *Principles of Economics.* Rev. ed. Homewood, Ill.: Richard D. Irwin, 1972. Excellent text reference for those interested in developing further understanding of basic economic principles. Chapters 17 and 18 relate to theory of economic growth and to economic growth and development. Valuable glossary of basic economic terms and phrases.

GUTMAN, PETER M., ed. *Economic Growth: An American Problem.* Englewood Cliffs, N.J.: Prentice-Hall, 1964. Excellent, very readable essays utilizing nontechnical terminology. Selections cover goals, growth, and policies for growth. Very fine source for those interested in obtaining quick insight into economic growth process.

SCHREIBER, ARTHUR F.; GATONS, PAUL K.; and CLEMMER, RICHARD B., eds. *Economics of Urban Problems: An Introduction.* Boston: Houghton Mifflin Co., 1971. First chapter deals with urban economic growth and location of jobs and people. Examines various aspects of overall demand and supply, technology, and urban factors as they relate to growth.

SCHULTZ, THEODORE W. "Investment in Human Capital." *American Economic Review* 51, no. 1 (March, 1961). Classic study of role of human capital in economic development. Clearly and forcefully presents returns society may obtain from investing in individuals.

CHAPTER 3

Demand for Education

Throughout the history of the United States there has been an almost continually increasing demand for education. The demand has gone through several transitions. In the Colonial period it was met largely by private institutions. Subsequent to Thomas Jefferson's presidency, those seeking educational services turned to public education supported by philanthropic contributions and land grants. Some of the latter sources still produce enormous revenue for public education. After the Reconstruction period, the demand for increased secondary and vocational education dominated the scene. The G.I. Bill of World War II gave the masses an opportunity for higher education and most colleges and universities experienced enormous growth. Starting in the late 1950s and up into the 1970s, community junior colleges and state-supported urban universities were built to handle millions of students who wanted to live near the institutions in which they were acquiring an education.

DEMOGRAPHIC FACTORS INFLUENCING DEMAND

Demography is the study of populations in relation to vital and social statistics. This section is concerned with the diverse clientele of American society and their educational accomplishments and aspirations. In 1970 there were over 60 million Americans attending schools and colleges. Since this represents a number of people far in excess of the populations of the vast majority of the world's nations, it is not surprising that the group was extremely heterogeneous. Table 3.1 shows the levels of this population's enrollment and the source of financial support for the institutions they attended. Obviously, such a mass of people will place widely divergent demands on educational institutions. Making the change essential to meeting these diverse demands is one way of maintaining healthy, evolving institutions. Private schools have more freedom to modify their offerings than do public schools; among institutions of higher learning, the community junior college generally is the most adaptable.

TABLE 3.1
EDUCATIONAL ENROLLMENTS, BY LEVEL AND TYPE OF INSTITUTION, 1970

Type of Institution	Number Enrolled (in thousands)	Females	Males
Public Elementary	27,497		
Private Elementary	4,200		
Total Elementary	31,697		
Public Secondary	18,407		
Private Secondary	1,400		
Total Secondary	19,807		
Public Higher Education	6,371		
Private Higher Education	2,127		
Total Higher Education	8,498	3,507	4,991
Total at All Levels	60,002		

SOURCE: *Statistical Abstract of the United States: 1971*, pp. 116, 127.

Does the part of the country in which a person resides have any relationship to whether or not he enrolls in a public or private institution?

Table 3.2 clearly indicates that a person born in the Middle Atlantic, New England, or East North Central states is far more likely to acquire his education in a private institution. In Pennsylvania a substantial portion of K–12 education is in private institutions. Such programs significantly

TABLE 3.2
REGIONAL VARIATIONS IN SCHOOL ENROLLMENTS
Fall 1970

	Percentage Enrolled in			
Section of Country	Public El.	Private El.	Public Sec.	Private Sec.
Middle Atlantic	76.2	23.8	88.4	11.6
New England	82.9	17.1	86.6	13.4
East North Central	83.7	16.3	91.3	8.7
Pacific	90.6	9.4	94.7	5.3
Southwest	93.0	7.0	97.1	2.9

SOURCE: *Statistical Abstract of the United States: 1971*, p. 116.

TABLE 3.3

YEARS OF SCHOOL COMPLETED, BY SEX
1957–59, 1970, and Projections to 1980

Year and Sex	Persons 25 Years and Over (in thousands)	Percent Completing This Many Years							
		None	1–4	5–7	8	9–11	12	13–15	16 or more
Female:									
1957–59	50,141	2.2	5.6	12.5	17.4	18.4	30.2	7.8	5.9
1970	57,527	1.3	3.4	8.8	13.1	18.0	37.5	9.7	8.2
1980 Proj.	67,123	0.7	2.2	6.2	9.0	18.0	42.1	11.2	10.7
1970 Accumulated frequency right to left		100.0	98.7	95.3	86.5	73.4	55.4	17.9	8.2
Male:									
1957–59 Av.	46,962	2.5	7.4	13.3	18.3	17.8	22.9	7.8	9.9
1970	51,784	1.3	4.5	9.4	13.6	16.1	30.1	10.8	14.1
1980 Proj.	63,243	0.7	2.9	6.2	8.9	16.8	36.3	11.2	16.9
1970 Accumulated frequency right to left		99.9+	98.6	94.1	84.7	71.1	55.0	24.9	14.1

SOURCE: *Statistical Abstract of the United States: 1971*, p. 109.

reduce the need for public expenditure for education. In Pennsylvania some schools are presently running half-day programs to avoid building expenses. Any effort by the proprietors of private institutions to turn the total burden for public education over to the local community and state government would create a crisis of large magnitude for school districts. In Pennsylvania, however, if such large numbers of students were not educated in private schools it is also possible that tax levies and bond proposals would find a more receptive public. If public money were made available for private schools, it is possible that such institutions, operating under fewer legal and legislative restrictions, would experiment with programs and technology in order to find ways in which educational productivity can be increased. Apparently private institutions as a whole are educating as well as the public ones. A strong demand for both public and private education continues in some parts of the nation.

The burden for K–12 education falls unevenly on states because some require longer terms than others and because the five- to seventeen-year-old age group is percentage-wise unevenly apportioned among the states. Maine has an average school term of 181.2 days, whereas in Vermont the term averages 171.8 days. This is a large discrepancy when dealing with thousands of students. Only 24.7 percent of Vermont's population is between five and seventeen years of age, while 30.5 percent of Mississippi's is. Geographic location is related to demand for education.

The data in Table 3.3 are informative about that part of the U.S. population that was born prior to 1948 and, to a fairly large degree, has completed its formal education. The 1970 accumulated rows provide information on the percentage of the over-twenty-five age group that has completed various years of schooling. They indicate that between grades four and eleven boys are more likely than girls to leave school; however, a major reversal occurs between the beginning and the end of grade twelve. A large number of girls in this age group either marry or become pregnant and leave school. While more females complete high school than males, a smaller percentage enter higher education and a significantly smaller percentage finish college. The Department of Commerce predictions for 1980 anticipate little change in this discrepancy. These data indicate that the sex of a student has some influence on the demands made for education.

RACE AND ETHNIC FACTORS

Ability is defined in this section as the possession of enough skill to accomplish a task. Success in formal education is significantly correlated with demonstrated ability on broadly standardized achievement tests in

TABLE 3.4

MEDIAN SCORES ON ACHIEVEMENT TESTS OF GRADE-1 AND GRADE-12 STUDENTS, 1965

Grade and Type of Test	White	Black	Puerto Rican	American Indian	Mexican-American	Oriental-American
Grade 1: Nonverbal	54.1	43.4	45.8	53.0	50.1	56.6
Verbal	53.2	45.4	44.9	47.8	46.5	51.6
Grade 12: Nonverbal	52.0	40.9	43.3	47.1	45.0	51.6
Verbal	52.1	40.9	43.1	43.7	43.8	49.6
Reading	51.9	42.2	42.6	44.3	44.2	48.8
Math	51.8	41.8	43.7	45.9	45.5	51.3
General Info.	52.2	40.6	41.7	44.7	43.3	49.0
Average Five Tests	52.0	41.1	43.1	45.1	44.4	50.1

SOURCE: *Statistical Abstract of the United States: 1971*, p. 119.

verbal and quantitative skills. Table 3.4 reveals that the median scores for whites surpass those of any minority group in both grade one and grade twelve, except for the Oriental Americans' edge in nonverbal skills in grade one. This indicates that whites are generally better equipped to cope with formal educational instruction both at the beginning and the end of their time in public schools. Since people usually want to do more of those things at which they are successful, it is not surprising that whites create a larger per capita demand for education than any minority group.

LITERACY A FACTOR IN EDUCATIONAL DEMAND

Persons are classified as illiterate if they cannot read or write in any language. Studies show that minority groups in the United States have a higher percentage of illiteracy than whites, but also that the percentage is becoming less each year for all groups, with a much greater diminution for minority groups. In 1959 1.6 percent of whites and 7.5 percent of the minority population over fourteen years of age were illiterate, whereas in 1969 only 0.7 percent of whites and 3.6 percent of the minority population over fourteen years of age were illiterate. An examination of the two age groups indicates that the discrepancy may disappear in a few more decades. Among whites sixty-five years and over, 5.1 percent in 1959 and 2.3 percent in 1969 were illiterate, while among minorities 25.5 percent were illiterate in 1959 and 16.7 percent in 1969. Similarly, among whites fourteen to twenty-four years of age, 0.5 percent were illiterate in 1959 and 0.2 percent in 1969, while among minorities fourteen to twenty-four years of age 1.2 percent were illiterate in 1959 and 0.5 percent in 1969. These data tend to indicate that illiteracy is more a function of when one was born than of race or ethnic group.

TABLE 3.5

ILLITERACY, BY AGE AND RACE

Age Group	Percentage Illiterate			
	1959		1969	
	White	Minority	White	Minority
Over 14	1.6	7.5	0.7	3.6
14–24	0.5	1.2	0.2	0.5
Over 65	5.1	25.5	2.3	16.7

SOURCE: *Statistical Abstract of the United States: 1971*, p.112.

Table 3.5 partly reveals why adult literacy programs are of special value to minority groups that were not encouraged to become literate at an earlier period in American history. A slightly smaller percentage of females are illiterate than are males in both white and minority groups, but again the discrepancy is being lessened with time. Right-to-read and adult education programs are lessening this problem. The operation of such programs created a demand for more educational services, which must be financed.

INCOME RELATED TO EDUCATIONAL DEMAND

Is income related to the level of education people attain? As shown by the data in Table 3.6, there appears to be a very high correlation between income and the level of educational attainment. For both blacks and whites, for every increase in educational attainment, there is an increase in salary; however, the increases for blacks are a great deal smaller at the upper levels than they are for whites. The acquisition of a college degree has been a way out of poverty for many ethnic groups, but starting in 1969 the effect of a college degree began to wane. If this trend continues, perhaps there will be less demand by the masses for higher education leading to a professional degree.

TABLE 3.6

MEDIAN INCOME AND EDUCATIONAL ATTAINMENTS OF MEN AGED 25–54

Formal Education	Median Income 1969		
	Black	White	All Races
Elementary: Total	$3,259	$ 4,529	$ 4,285
Less than 8 years	2,973	3,613	3,429
8 years	4,293	5,460	5,345
High School: Total	4,748	7,890	7,578
1–3 years	5,222	7,309	7,079
4 years	6,144	8,613	8,434
College: 1 or more years	8,567	12,437	12,255

SOURCE: *The Official Associated Press Almanac, 1973* (New York: Almanac Publishing Co., 1972), p. 375.

MIGRATION AND ITS EFFECT ON HIGHER EDUCATION

Apparently many people feel they can acquire a better or easier education outside of their native state. At times this may reflect a lack of effort on the part of the home state to provide higher education, and the migration of students puts an additional burden on the resources of other states. Another way of viewing this is that some states offer educational opportunities that attract many students from other states. The per capita wealth of citizens in some states is such that they can afford to send students out of state for an education. Some states have a larger percentage of high-prestige institutions that attract students from many areas. Table 3.7 shows several of these relationships.

States in Group A have a large percentage of students leaving the state for an education. Group B has about the same percentage leaving and entering. Group C has a large percentage of students entering the state for an education. Group D has a small percentage leaving the state as well as entering it for an education. If the difference between emigration and immigration is a large positive number, this might indicate a paucity of higher-education opportunity, an unpleasant higher-educational situation, or that a lot of money is available to send students out of state. In the latter case, there may be a lessened higher-education opportunity for the poor. If the difference is a large negative number, this may indicate an abundance of educational opportunity, the existence of several prestigious institutions, availability of inexpensive higher education, or low per capita wealth.

The states in Groups B and D show a well-balanced emigration-immigration. Texas and California both represent states with large populations that are surrounded by less populous states. Both have large numbers enrolled in higher education and consequently a sizable influx from adjacent states would cause little change in the percentage enrolled. Both New Mexico and Ohio are near large-population states with abundant higher-educational resources. The slight difference in emigration and immigration in these states probably results from an overflow of students from nearby large-population states. Furthermore, a sizable number appear to leave those states to avail themselves of excellent education facilities just across the border.

Table 3.8 presents enrollment of college-age students for selected states. The percentage of potential college students enrolled in higher education in New Jersey compares favorably with that of Texas, and the percentage enrolled in Connecticut compares favorably with California. However, both Connecticut and New Jersey depend on other states providing their students opportunities for higher education. The fact that both Connecticut and New Jersey have high per capita incomes may also

TABLE 3.7
Students Moving from State to State for Higher Education, 1958–68

Group	State of Residence	Percentage Emigrating from Home State 1958	1963	1968	Percentage Immigrating to New State 1958	1963	1968	Percentage Difference 1958	1963	1968
A	Ala.	32	52	48	10	14	19	22	33	29
	N.J.	42	42	47	12	12	11	30	30	36
	Del.	48	50	42	37	38	40	11	12	2
	Conn.	39	39	38	25	22	21	14	17	17
	N.H.	35	39	37	52	57	53	−17	−18	−16
B	N.Mex.	21	22	17	20	24	17	−1	−2	0
	Ohio	16	16	15	20	20	18	0	−4	−3
C	Vt.	34	36	33	64	67	61	−30	−31	−28
	R.I.	31	31	28	48	46	37	−17	−15	−9
	Maine	31	31	30	38	37	36	−7	−6	−6
	Utah	6	5	4	35	35	32	−29	−30	−28
	Mass.	19	22	21	33	33	31	−14	−11	−10
D	Tex.	6	6	5	8	9	9	−2	−3	−4
	Calif.	6	5	5	9	6	6	−3	−1	−1

SOURCE: *A Fact Book on Higher Education* (Washington: American Council on Education, 1972), pp. 72.172–72.175.

TABLE 3.8
College-age Students Enrolled in Selected States, 1968

State	Age Group 13–24	Total Enrollment	Immigrating for Education	Emigrating for Education	$E = B + D - C$ Net Migration	Percentage Enrolled
Ala.	45,000	2,738	532	2,001	4,207	9.3
N.J.	729,000	122,863	13,549	98,270	207,584	22.3
Del.	63,000	11,290	4,510	4,929	11,709	18.6
Conn.	326,000	76,731	16,169	36,854	97,416	29.9
N.H.	86,000	21,587	11,356	6,091	16,322	19.0
Total	1,249,000	235,209	46,160	148,145	337,202	27.0
Mich.	1,031,000	249,513	28,928	15,979	236,564	22.9
La.	444,000	97,934	10,119	6,516	94,331	21.2
Calif.	2,447,000	708,614	39,291	35,405	704,728	28.8
Tex.	1,380,000	313,055	27,079	16,160	302,136	21.9
Utah	143,000	57,953	18,540	1,690	41,103	28.7
Total	5,445,000	1,427,069	123,957	75,750	1,378,862	25.3

SOURCE: *A Fact Book on Higher Education* (Washington: American Council on Education, 1972), pp. 72.172–72.175.

TABLE 3.9
INCREASE IN NUMBER OF EARNED ADVANCED DEGREES, 1949–70

Year	All Earned Degrees	Number of Master's Degrees	Percentage of all Degrees	Number of Doctor's Degrees	Percentage of all Degrees
1949–50	498,373	58,219	11.7	6,420	1.3
1959–60	479,215	74,497	15.5	9,829	2.1
1969–70	1,072,581	209,387	19.5	29,872	2.8

SOURCE: *A Fact Book on Higher Education* (Washington: American Council on Education, 1972), p. 72.189.

TABLE 3.10
EARNED ADVANCED DEGREES, 1949–70, BY SEX

| Year | Master's Degrees ||||| Doctor's Degrees |||||
| | Females || Males || Females || Males || Females ||
	Number	Percentage	Number	Percentage	Number	Percentage	Number	Percentage
1949–50	16,982	29.2	41,237	70.8	5,804	90.4	616	9.6
1959–60	23,560	31.6	50,937	68.4	8,801	39.5	1,028	10.5
1969–70	83,241	39.8	126,146	60.2	25,892	87.7	3,980	13.3

SOURCE: *A Fact Book on Higher Education* (Washington: American Council on Education, 1972), pp. 72.192–72.193.

indicate that more of the eighteen-to-twenty-four age-group have the ability to finance an education outside the state. A variety of factors interact to influence opportunity for acquiring an education, but nothing clear-cut can be said about a higher or lower percentage of students who receive a higher education simply because of the peculiarities of that state.

ABILITY AND ITS RELATIONSHIP TO OBTAINING ADVANCED DEGREES

A definite trend toward a larger percentage of students working toward and obtaining advanced degrees has been shown over the past two decades. Table 3.9 presents data on earned degrees for 1949–70. These data reveal that the number of people obtaining master's and doctor's degrees nearly tripled in the ten-year period between 1960 and 1970. Table 3.10 presents information on earned advanced degrees by sex. In 1950, 1960, and 1970 women earned respectively 24.4, 34.2, and 40.4 percent of all degrees. While females are still well behind males in the percentage that obtain college degrees, they are rapidly closing the gap. The story on advanced degrees is quite different. While females are acquiring an increasingly larger percentage of advanced degrees, they are only about half as likely to obtain a master's degree and only about one-sixth as likely to obtain a doctor's degree. Department of Health, Education, and Welfare regulations, as well as governmental laws, have created a large number of openings in institutions of higher education for all minority groups, including females who hold advanced degrees. The white Protestant male with good credentials and a recently acquired advanced degree may search in vain for a position, whereas the female or member of a minority group with the same qualifications is likely to be sought after by competing institutions. As increasingly larger numbers of females and members of minority groups become aware of the magnitude of this market, they are likely to demand opportunities and concessions that will enable them to obtain advanced degrees.

STATE POPULATION RELATED TO DEMAND FOR COLLEGE DEGREES

Is there a relationship between the population of a state and the number of people who obtain professional degrees?

The data in Table 3.11 show that persons in states with a small population obtain a larger percentage of degrees than the proportionate

TABLE 3.11

Relationship Between State Population and Number of Residents Obtaining Advanced Degrees

State	Percentage of Total U.S. Population	Percentage of Total Degrees	Percentage of Total Master's Degrees	Percentage of Total Doctor's Degrees
Calif.	9.8	8.9	9.1	10.4
N.Y.	9.0	9.6	12.9	10.5
Pa.	5.8	5.8	5.4	5.1
Tex.	5.5	4.9	4.1	4.2
Ill.	5.5	5.2	5.9	6.5
Ohio	5.2	5.0	4.2	4.4
Mich.	4.4	4.6	5.7	5.6
Total	45.2	44.0	47.3	46.7
Mont.	0.3	0.4	0.3	0.2
S.Dak.	0.3	0.5	0.4	0.2
N.Dak.	0.3	0.4	0.3	0.4
Del.	0.3	0.2	0.2	0.2
Nev.	0.2	0.1	0.1	0.1
Vt.	0.2	0.3	0.3	0.1
Wyo.	0.2	0.2	0.1	0.3
Total	1.8	2.1	1.7	1.5

Source: *The World Almanac, 1972* (Newspaper Enterprise Association, 1971), p. 46; *A Fact Book on Higher Education* (Washington: American Council on Education, 1972), pp. 72.198–72.217.

population of the state. When one examines the percentage of master's and doctor's degrees, however, the reverse is true. The number of advanced degrees awarded is more than the population justifies in states with large populations, but the overall figure for large states is apparently strongly influenced by the advanced degrees granted in New York and Michigan. At the doctor's level, Wyoming, the state with the second smallest population, has a higher ratio of its people obtaining doctorates than any of the large states. The fact that Ohio has a population three times that of the seven smallest states, yet produces nearly the same ratio of advanced degrees to population as the average for the small-population states, makes generalizations about population and advanced degrees difficult to defend.

NDEA TITLE IV GRADUATE FELLOWSHIPS AWARDED, BY GEOGRAPHIC LOCATION

Many students depend on NDEA Title IV Graduate Fellowships to finance their education. Is there a relationship between being a recipient of such a grant and residing in a particular state? In order to attempt to analyze this question, Table 3.12 has been constructed to show the relationship among small-, medium-, and large-population states.

TABLE 3.12

DISTRIBUTION OF NDEA TITLE IV GRADUATE FELLOWSHIPS, 1970

State	Population	NDEA Fellowship	10,000 times Ratio of Population to Fellowships
Hawaii	769,913	210	2.73
Ala.	302,173	16	0.53
N.Dak.	617,761	168	2.72
Idaho	713,008	107	1.50
S.C.	2,590,516	227	0.88
W.Va.	1,744,237	102	0.58
Iowa	2,825,041	582	2.06
Nebr.	1,483,791	222	1.50
Miss.	2,216,912	187	0.08
Fla.	6,789,443	795	1.17
N.J.	7,168,164	680	0.95
Ind.	5,193,669	1,113	2.14
Mass.	5,689,170	1,596	2.80

SOURCE: *A Fact Book on Higher Education* (Washington: American Council on Education, 1972), p. 72.163.

Apparently the percentage of NDEA fellowship recipients has no systematic relationship to the population of a state, but it is also true that a student in Massachusetts had a thirty-five-times greater opportunity of receiving an NDEA fellowship than a student in Mississippi. Possibly the existence of prestigious institutions, the political climate within a state, and the presence or absence of persons highly skilled in obtaining grants have contributed to disparities in awards.

POPULATION TRENDS IN METROPOLITAN CENTERS AFFECTING EDUCATIONAL DEMAND

The large metropolitan centers of the United States have changing patterns of population that create demands for educational modifications. The immigrant with high aspirations has fled to the suburbs, leaving the metropolitan areas populated by transient blacks and Spanish-surnamed ethnic groups. In order to function effectively in industry, many of the present minority groups must possess vocational and technical skills of much higher levels than were required of European immigrants during the last century. Educating for these skills is more expensive than providing academic programs, yet inner-city school districts are extremely hard pressed financially because of a simultaneous devaluation of taxable assets and inflation of operating costs. About one-half of the large cities have decreased in population during the past three decades. This usually means little new building construction. The net result has frequently been a continuous deterioration of educational services.

TABLE 3.13

DECREASING NUMBER OF WHITES LIVING IN URBAN CENTERS, 1900–70
(Percentage of Total Population)

City	1900	1940	1950	1960	1970
New York	98.2	93.9	90.5	86.0	81.0
Chicago	98.2	91.8	86.4	77.1	68.0
Philadelphia	95.2	87.0	81.8	73.6	68.0
Detroit	98.6	90.8	83.8	71.1	53.0
Washington	68.9	72.0	65.0	46.1	32.0
Atlanta	60.2	65.4	63.4	61.7	61.0
Montgomery	43.2	55.8	60.1	64.9	68.0

SOURCE: Robert J. Havighurst and Daniel V. Levine, *Education in Metropolitan Areas* (Boston: Allyn & Bacon, 1971), p. 210.

Table 3.13 shows a paradoxical situation in relationship to racial migration in metropolitan areas. Some northern cities show a decrease in population and all have a progressively smaller white population, while cities in the South have grown both in population and in the percentage of white inhabitants. The southern states, whose cities have a healthier economy, could make a larger expenditure for education, yet blacks are leaving this part of the country and migrating to an area where schools can less easily supply their needs for an education. It may be that the larger northern and Pacific Coast metropolitan centers have the political power to utilize federal funds for solving their educational dilemma, which had long been a problem for the less politically powerful South. For additional information on educational demands in urban areas, read the book by Havighurst and Levine noted as the source for Table 3.13.

EMPLOYMENT AS AN EDUCATIONAL DEMAND

The data in Table 3.14 indicate that the high school graduate, regardless of race or sex, is less likely to be unemployed than the high school dropout. During 1970 the possibility of unemployment was greater than in 1965 for all sixteen- to twenty-one-year-olds, regardless of sex or race, but was nearly twice as frequent among high school dropouts. The minority person who was a high school dropout had about one chance in three of being unemployed. These data clearly indicate that sixteen- to twenty-one-year-olds should remain in school until they acquire a salable skill. One reason for the increased unemployment for this age group in 1970 as compared to 1965 is the increasing technical skills needed in work. Young people today need intensive training in technical and vocational fields if they are to avoid the hazards of unemployment.

GEOGRAPHIC LOCATION RELATED TO YEARS OF SCHOOLING COMPLETED

People reared in the Mountain and Pacific Coast states remain in school for 12.0 or more years. This is a significantly longer period than is found in other sections of the country. The highly urbanized states, with the exception of California, are about average in holding power, while the "Confederate States," except for Florida and Texas, generally have a population with fewer than nine years of formal education. While much of this can be attributed to a former paucity of formal educational opportunities for blacks (average attainment 6.0 years), the whites in this section also demand fewer years of school than whites in most other parts of the nation.

GOVERNMENTAL REGULATIONS AND EDUCATIONAL DEMAND

Between 1940 and 1970 the federal government spent over $167 billion for veterans' benefits. In 1970 alone over $9 billion was spent for veterans' benefits. A large portion of this money was funneled directly into

TABLE 3.14
UNEMPLOYMENT AMONG HIGH SCHOOL GRADUATES AND DROPOUTS AGED 16–21

Year	Percentage of Graduates Unemployed					Percentage of Dropouts Unemployed				
	Total	Female	Male	Minority	White	Total	Female	Male	Minority	White
1965	8.4	9.9	6.5	15.0	7.7	14.9	19.7	12.6	19.0	14.7
1970	11.6	11.2	12.0	24.6	10.6	21.5	21.8	21.4	31.3	18.7

SOURCE: *Statistical Abstract of the United States: 1971*, p. 112.

education. The insurance paid to widows and orphans frequently was also utilized for educational purposes. Two five-year periods occurred when the large influx of veterans into institutions of higher education created major logistical problems for these institutions. Immediately following World War II, in 1945–49, the federal government provided funds for education amounting to $7.7 billion, and in the 1950–54 period, when Korean veterans returned to school, the federal government supported educational efforts in an amount in excess of $7 billion. These governmental expenditures contributed to solving a severe teacher shortage that existed during the decades of the 1950s and 1960s. The educational provisions of the G.I. Bill supplied money for thousands of Korean veterans to finance advanced degrees. The value of these degrees was soon apparent since they provided the large increase in faculty so essential to staffing the institutions of higher education during the late fifties and throughout the sixties when huge masses of students began to pursue college degrees. As a result of U.S. embarrassment when *Sputnik* was launched, a major program was created to provide this nation with more scientific brain-power. The federal government, in cooperation with the National Science Foundation, sponsored year-long and summer institutes designed to improve science-teaching and science-training in this country. These programs were highly successful and so effective that by 1970 the nation had a large surplus of highly qualified scientists, whose numbers so increased during the 1970–73 period that concern is now being shown about the abundance of unemployed and underemployed scientists. Some feel the federal government might wisely invest in supporting these scientists while they investigate many of the maladies of mankind.

Presidents Kennedy and Johnson particularly engineered major programs aimed at providing minority groups with opportunities to enjoy more fully the great abundance of the American economy. Three of the larger and more successful efforts were National Defense Student Loans (NDSL), Educational Opportunity Grants, and the College Work-Study Programs. Between 1959 and 1968, 1,863,513 students in the United States availed themselves of $1,058,821,000 in National Defense Student Loans. Table 3.15 shows the number of students and the amount of money pumped into education by a few of the governmental programs. Certainly the expenditure of over $700 million on education by the federal government in 1970 increased demand for educational services. Most of the programs were written in such a manner that institutions and individuals had to exhibit a willingness to pay for part of the program; consequently, the actual amount of money brought into education by such governmental activities was magnified. Additional information on how much was spent in each state can be found in the reference source to Table 3.15.

TABLE 3.15
SOME EXAMPLES OF FEDERAL SUPPORT FOR EDUCATION, FISCAL 1972

	Type of Support			
	National Defense Student Loans	Educational Opportunity Grants	College Work-Study Program	Total for These Programs
Number of students utilizing	648,900	297,300	545,000	1,491,200
Dollar expenditure for	$286,000,000	$177,337,000	$237,228,000	$700,565,000
Average expenditure per student	$440.75	$596.49	$437.12	$469.80

SOURCE: *A Fact Book on Higher Education* (Washington: American Council on Education, 1972), pp. 72.164–72.169.

SUMMARY

The purpose of this chapter has been to investigate demographic and economic factors that have created or will create a demand for educational services. It appears that the changes during the next decade will largely result from attempts to correct the inequalities of educational and job opportunities that now exist in this country. The new demands for educational services most likely to occur are: (1) increased opportunity and support for females to obtain advanced degrees; (2) a change in high school and junior college education resulting in more salable technical and vocational skills; (3) special programs to assist minority groups in acquiring additional representation in higher education; (4) adult education programs to cope with economic debilitations such as illiteracy and vocational obsolescence; and (5) an international effort to help people understand that the solutions to such ominous problems as planet pollution, intolerance, and food and energy shortages can only result from individuals making a personal commitment to solving them, through a demonstrated willingness to be informed and to sacrifice some of their own luxuries, pleasures, and conveniences.

BIBLIOGRAPHY

American Council on Education. *A Fact Book on Higher Education.* Third Issue, Washington, 1972. Deals with institutions, faculty and staff, and student characteristics and finances. Has abundance of materials on students migrating into and out of various states, as well as excellent tables on financial resources of institutions, faculty salaries, fellowships awarded, and tuition charged by states, and information on international education.
―――. *A Fact Book on Higher Education.* Fourth Issue, Washington, 1972. Provides comprehensive overview of degrees awarded in United States since 1949. National maps give rapid overview of degrees in nation. Also provides breakdown of degrees from Associate of Arts through Doctor of Philosophy. Excellent reference for male-female ratios as related to various levels and types of degree. Detailed breakdowns by state, region, and area of specialization.
Educational Testing Service. *Guide to the Use of GRE Scores in Graduate Admissions, 1971–1972.* Princeton, N.J., 1972. Describes advanced tests in special subject-matter areas. Provides data for analyzing scores and speculates on failure of such tests to measure fairly all ethnic and minority groups.
O'NEILL, JUNE. *Resource Use in Higher Education.* Berkeley: Carnegie Commission on Higher Education, 1971. Provides information on enrollments as far back as 1890. Contains many line graphs depicting educational phenomena.

Focuses attention on enrollment compared to gross national product and population in 18–21 age-group. Also describes cost of education for four decades in constant and current dollars. Excellent section of up-to-date references in higher education.

CHAPTER 4

Supply of Educational Services

The largest single economic unit in a vast majority of the towns and cities of this country is the public school system and/or the higher education institution located therein. In many political subdivisions of limited natural and industrial resources, the schools are the major source of external income. Federal and state funds provide salaries for administrators, bus drivers, custodians, and teachers, and these are largely expended on purchases of goods and services in the local area. Because the educational system has such a major impact on the economy of any political subdivision in which it is located, its ceasing to operate, and the accompanying diminution of money available in the area, may necessitate major changes in the local economy. Since school closings have so often struck a death-blow to small-town economies, many such towns have fought against the consolidation of schools in their area. There is no doubt, however, that if the schools educate well, the result will be a citizenry who have the imagination and skills necessary for the production of higher-quality, and perhaps less expensive goods and services.

In Chapter 2 it was pointed out that expenditures for all levels of public and private education in this country amounted to over $75 billion, or approximately 7.7 percent of the gross national product. This chapter deals with the allocation of these expenditures and the marketing of educational services. "Formal education or schooling is the product of a surplus economy."[1] The huge investment in education made by the American economy is even more spectacular in view of the fact that it comes entirely from the surplus economy.

COSTS OF PROVIDING EDUCATION

At nearly every level of education the major item of expenditure is faculty salaries. Few informed people would deny that the overall formal

1. John S. Brubacher, *A History of the Problems of Education* (New York: McGraw-Hill Book Co., 1947), p. 75.

education of students completing high school and college programs today is far superior to that of the past. The quality has improved, but teachers still instruct about the same number of students they have for the past 125 years. A farmer today produces from five to ten times as many goods as he did in 1850, carpenters build houses faster, and secretaries produce significantly more composition, but a teacher still averages from twenty to thirty full-time student equivalents. Since productivity has not kept pace with salaries paid, education requires a larger chunk of the gross national product each year. The reader is encouraged to examine Chapter 1 of Benson's book,[2] if he wishes a more extensive discussion of the processes of economic decision-making in educational matters.

Fifty years ago, Dr. Ben Pittenger wrote that the items of major importance in school finance were: (1) the growth of public school expenditures; (2) the enormous cost of education; (3) the reaction against high taxes; (4) a crisis in school finance; and (5) a fictitious rise in school costs.[3] Ellwood P. Cubberly, in his introduction to Pittenger's book, made the following statement:

With our rapidly multiplying population, the expansion upward and outward of instruction offered a pronounced increase in attendance in the upper and more expensive levels, the many new demands being made on the schools, the extension of and increase in the costs for all forms of government, the struggle with other city departments for funds, and the general breakdown of the old real and personal property taxes as a means of governmental support, the question of educational cost was certain to become one of vital importance had no war come along to force the problem almost at once, into bold relief.

Apparently the problem of financing education has been around for at least fifty years. There are no perfect models or even universally acceptable designs in school finance. In most cases planning begins with a budget, and a statement of desired goals. The planning for financing a school operation must consider the particular requirements of the system. A rapidly expanding district near a major city will have to utilize large amounts of money for creating new facilities, so its capital outlay will be high. An older district that is not growing may find it wise to invest more in maintenance of its facilities so they can be used for longer periods of time. Some school systems, which have large numbers of experienced and highly competent teachers, will want to invest a large portion of their income in faculty salaries with a minimal portion for supervision. A new

2. Charles S. Benson, *The Economics of Public Education* (New York: Houghton Mifflin Co., 1968).
3. Benjamin F. Pittenger, *An Introduction to Public School Finance* (Boston: Houghton-Mifflin Co., 1925).

school district may have a large number of inexperienced and fairly young teachers, in which case it would be obligated for less in teachers' salaries, but perhaps more for supervision and equipment acquisition. Tables 4.1 and 4.2 show the average distribution of school funds over a large number of districts; they are not intended to be used as a standard against which any particular district should evaluate itself.

TABLE 4.1

UTILIZATION OF PUBLIC SCHOOL (K-12) FUNDS, 1963-64

School Expenditure	Amount (In Millions of Dollars)	Percentage of Total
Instructional Salaries	10,711	50.2
Capital Outlay	2,978	14.0
Operation of Plant	1,446	6.8
School Services (cafeteria, health, attendance, etc.)	1,394	6.5
Fixed charges (teacher retirement, social security, etc.)	1,344	6.3
Instructional Supplies and Services	1,039	4.9
Administration	745	3.5
Interest	701	3.3
Maintenance of Plant	539	2.5
Community Services (extension, summer school, etc.)	428	2.0
Total	21,325	100.0

SOURCE: Charles S. Benson, *The Economics of Public Education* (New York: Houghton Mifflin Co., 1968), p. 14.

The largest single expenditure for every level of schooling is faculty salaries. It is so significant that C. C. Colvert has created a formula for budgeting junior college expenditures on the basis of faculty salaries, which is utilized by many junior college administrators. Because such a large portion of the budget is devoted to faculty salaries, it is the most difficult item to increase significantly without a large increase in organizational income. Salaries are the easiest component to adjust downward a few hundred dollars if the administration wants to add a new facility or service. During 1971-72, according to National Education Association estimates, 1,138,418 elementary teachers received an average of income of $9,420 and 951,204 secondary teachers earned an average income of $10,015. This represented an expenditure for teachers of over $20 billion,

TABLE 4.2
UTILIZATION OF HIGHER EDUCATION FUNDS, 1950–68
(In Millions of Dollars)

Item of Expense	1950	1960	1968	Percentage of Total (1968)
Instruction and Departmental Research	781	1,793	5,139	25.3
Plant Expansion	417	1,192	3,786	18.7
Organized Research	225	1,022	2,699	13.3
Auxiliary Enterprises	476	916	2,302	11.4
Administration and General	213	583	1,739	8.6
Organized Activities Related to Instruction	119	303	1,155	5.7
Plant Operation and Maintenance	225	470	1,127	5.6
Libraries and Public Services	143	341	1,091	5.4
Scholarships, Fellowships, Prizes	63	172	713	3.5
Miscellaneous			516	2.5
Total	2,246	5,601	20,276	100.9

SOURCE: *Statistical Abstract of the United States: 1971*, p. 126.

or 43.4 percent of the total expenditure for elementary and secondary education.

Faculty salaries are also the largest item of expenditure for institutions of higher education. During 1971–72 colleges and universities spent about $12.3 billion for 954,000 faculty members, whose average annual salaries were $12,923.[4] Faculty salaries, including research support, represented 43.6 percent of the total expenditures for higher education in the United States. It is interesting to note that the percentage of total expenditures for faculty salaries is virtually the same for public K–12 education as it is for higher education, despite the fact that vastly different clienteles with very diverse needs are served by the two levels.

From a strictly economic point of view, it is necessary for all educational institutions to produce more students per faculty member if they are to enjoy noninflationary salary increases. The fact that education at all levels is utilizing over twice the percentage of the gross national product that it was four decades ago, without an attendant improvement in

---
4. *A Fact Book on Higher Education* (Washington: American Council on Education, 1972), p. 72.140.

student-faculty ratio, probably indicates that education is partially responsible for the inflation this country has experienced. If the research and/or the students produced lead to accelerated production in other segments of the economy, equal to or greater than the increased part of the gross national product education receives, then education has not created inflationary pressures.

It is interesting that only 25.3 percent of the expenditures in higher education were for instruction. The typical citizen usually pictures the university as a place where one goes to learn. As the population bulge moves up the formal-education ladder, it may be possible to divert the 18.7 percent of the budget presently allocated for plant expansion to more educationally productive efforts. The fact that 8.6 percent of the budget was spent for administration tempts one to speculate on why one administrator is necessary for every three teachers in an institution of higher education, while in public education one administrator can cope with fourteen teachers of supposedly less competence.

CAPITAL

All educational institutions must make periodic expenditures for purchasing new or replacing worn-out equipment. These are somewhat predictable and should be planned. Public schools in areas of expanding population and many institutions of higher education are carrying out almost perpetual building programs. Between 1950 and 1965 about 68,000 new K–12 classrooms were added each year.[5] The price per classroom averaged $49,000 in 1966. Many institutions of learning are remodeling to meet changing building codes and are adding structural features that make getting an education a more comfortable pursuit. Changing patterns of where people live have caused many large schools to build new structures away from the central city and to abandon usable buildings in the central city. All the foregoing considerations are responsible for school districts and institutions of higher education buying land on which to build, revamping existing structures, and adding to the permanent equipment used in carrying out the educational mission. These capital-outlay expenditures are provided from current revenues, gifts, or borrowing, and in 1963–64 amounted to 14.0 percent of the educational budget. While Table 4.3 shows an increase in dollars spent in eight of the ten years, it should be noted that there was a decrease in the percentage of total expenditures designated for capital outlays over the decade. The three

5. Robert J. Garvue, *Modern Public School Finance* (New York: Macmillan, 1969), p. 192.

TABLE 4.3
Capital Outlay Expenditures by School Systems, 1959–70

School Year	Capital Outlay Expenditures (in Thousands of Dollars)	Percentage of Change Over 1959–60	Percentage of Change Over Previous Period	Percentage of Total Educational Expenditure
1959–60	2,661,786	—	—	17.0
1961–62	2,862,153	7.5	+7.5	—
1962–63	3,130,697	17.6	+9.4	17.0
1963–64	2,977,976	11.9	−4.9	17.0
1964–65	3,241,285	21.8	+8.8	15.2
1965–66	3,754,862	41.1	+15.8	16.3
1966–67	3,662,106	37.6	−2.5	12.9
1967–68	4,105,512	54.2	+12.1	12.9
1968–69	4,461,140	67.6	+8.7	12.5
1969–70	4,709,853	76.9	+5.6	11.9

SOURCE: *Financial Status of the Public Schools, 1970* (Washington: National Education Association, Committee on Educational Finance, 1970), p. 44.

factors that have contributed to this decline are: (1) the reduction in first-graders entering school; (2) the reluctance of taxpayers to increase their obligations; and (3) some diminution in the number of people moving to suburbs.

EQUIPMENT

Private enterprise will often employ a specialist for $10,000 and provide him with $100,000 worth of equipment to enable him to operate as efficiently as possible. Professional education, on the other hand, will employ a specialist for $10,000 and then, typically, demonstrate a reluctance to provide even $200 per faculty member for the equipment, materials, and supplies that would enable him to be productive. The only basis for such conduct by educational administrators and the general public seems to be that historically all a teacher at any level needed to work with was a piece of chalk, a chalkboard, and a textbook. Instructional supplies and services, as itemized in Table 4.1, account for only 4.9 percent of the educational budget. With a substantial portion of that being utilized in providing library or learning-resource-center personnel and expendable supplies, it is apparent that faculty members have very limited resources for improving individual productivity. In most cases equipment and supplies amount to less than 5 percent of salary expenditures or 2 percent of the educational budget.

As teaching evolves into a more demanding profession, it would appear that a five-fold increase to 10 percent of the educational budget for instructional supplies and services might be justified. The administration and public have a right to expect this added assistance to teachers to be noninflationary, and justifiably are entitled to know how such a step can be financed. It could be accomplished by increasing the student-faculty ratio at all levels from the current 17.4:1 to about 18.8:1. The change in support could be incremental over a period of eight years without seriously disrupting the system.

How would the additional $1,839 per teacher [(8.0 percent/42.5 percent) ($10,000) = $1,839] be expended? Five hundred hours (12 hours per week) of clerical help could be employed for $839 to alleviate some of the menial tasks of teaching, and would provide on the average for all levels [(12 hr./17.4) (60 minutes per hour) = 41.3 minutes] 41.3 minutes of additional time each week for each student. The remaining $1,000 per year, if utilized wisely over a period of eight years, could provide the teacher with a private study area, a private desk, tape recorders, calculators, typewriters, and other gadgetry that would enable him to become more productive, so that he could educate 18.8 students at least as effectively as he previously had educated 17.4 students.

MATERIALS

While equipment includes those items that will be used repeatedly over a period of several years, materials are expendable items that must be replenished regularly. Something less than 2 percent of the educational budget is spent on items such as pencils, ditto paper, books, chalk, and ink. A sufficient supply of these materials has a positive effect on faculty morale, while rationing may be utilized as an excuse for operating ineffectively and inefficiently. If the system is large, it is possible to receive substantial discounts on mass purchases. This requires a logistical system that can identify the material needs of a large number of people, consolidate such lists, make the purchases, and store the materials until the proper time for distribution to the users.

A faculty of 4,000 might utilize as much as 200,000 reams of ditto paper in one year. If the paper weighs three pounds per ream, purchased at a cost of $1.30 each, this means a $260,000 purchase that will weigh 300 tons and require six semi-trailers to carry it. If individual purchases were made at $2 per ream, the increased cost to the system would be $140,000. Faculty members should be made aware that such an unessential expenditure, caused by not planning purchases in advance, results in less money for salaries and other instructional materials.

Some states provide the pencils and paper that children are expected to use. What does this mean in a school district with 40,000 students? Assume each child is issued two writing tablets and two pencils each month during the school year. The district is able to mass-purchase the pencils at $0.0225 ($2\frac{1}{4}$¢) each and the tablets at $0.085 ($8\frac{1}{2}$¢) each. The pencils cost $0.05 and the writing tablets $0.15 in local stores. What savings result from this single larger-scale purchase?

Cost of pencils   20 pencils/child × 40,000 children × $0.0225 per pencil = $18,000

Cost of writing tablets   20 tablets/child × 40,000 children × $0.085 per tablet = $68,000

This represents a savings of $74,000 over local purchases, but if the school had not provided these materials, local purchases would have produced $160,000 more in local business. Would the money individual parents spent on pencils and writing tablets in districts where these are not provided become a part of the area economy? If the materials were provided by the district, would the savings to parents have been invested in some other more magnifying facet of the local economy? Obviously there exists no simple answer applicable to all levels of educational institutions.

Colleges and universities have their own stores for materials, which are in competition with local retailers. Increasingly, larger high schools are also developing similar goods outlets. Such an economic unit may do hundreds of thousands of dollars of business annually. Should prices be low enough to negate the possibility of profit? Should the store make a profit, which could be used to aid the educationally needy or to provide more student services? These too are difficult questions to answer.

OBSOLESCENCE

Educational institutions are affected by obsolescence of equipment, of the programs they offer, and of the skills of their employees. In order to minimize the cost of providing up-to-date equipment, an institution must have personnel who can modify existing equipment, keep aware of what is new and worthwhile on the market, purchase durable equipment, and budget for predictable replacements. This is almost identical to the problems faced by any economic unit, except that an educational institution probably has more diverse equipment than most businesses.

In order to avoid obsolescence in programs, educational institutions must critically evaluate both the internal and the external milieus. Are there societal needs that justify the existence of certain programs? Are the employees utilizing their skills effectively and efficiently in helping learners move toward the attainment of societal goals for the institution? Surveys analyzing the community, jobs, student aspirations, courses of study, and post-graduation follow-up of students, as well as regular perusal of educational research, can all assist in ascertaining whether or not programs are becoming obsolete. Such efforts are analogous to production and marketing surveys in a noneducational economic unit.

Probably the worst thing that can happen to an educational institution is for its faculty to become obsolete. This is most likely to happen when an institution is not growing and therefore does not have the continuous infusion of new ideas and enthusiasm typical of an expanding institution. In order to avoid such obsolescence an institution can employ people with professional dedication and then provide opportunities for them to learn. In several states, both in public schools and in institutions of higher education, there are provisions for sabbatical leave. A faculty member may also become eligible for a paid leave as early as five years or at a period longer than the seven-year sabbatical, which is most common. There are many policies for the implementation of such leaves. A teacher may receive full salary for one semester or half-salary for a school year. Generally, he will promise to return to the same place of employment for at least one year after completing such a leave. The leave time may be used by the faculty member to write a book, to carry on educational travel, to return to the classroom for additional formal education, to study, or to serve as a guest teacher or professor at some other educational institution. The expenditures for sabbatical leaves can be justified by the granting institutions in several ways: as a reward for loyal and worthy service, or on the basis that such an experience will rekindle the enthusiasm of a teacher, who may then serve as a catalyst for stimulating other faculty members into creating a vibrant learning atmosphere in the school. Junior colleges can use the sabbatical opportunity to increase the educational level of their faculty in order to meet increasingly higher educational standards set forth by accreditation agencies.

An outstanding scholar at a private university may write a book that becomes a best-seller or accept a high government position, either of which can bring prestige to the granting institution, thereby causing more students to want to matriculate at that institution. Ultimately, the economic return depends on the recipient's professional performance. If he is not committed and dedicated to fulfilling his obligation, when granted the opportunity to improve his skills, the money may not be well spent.

INFLATION AND INTEREST

Inflation and interest are treated together because of the significant interrelationship between them in financing educational opportunities. Government at all levels is increasingly incurring indebtedness which is to be defrayed by future revenues. The combined local-, state-, and federal-government indebtedness at the end of fiscal year 1966 was estimated to be $427 billion, or a six-fold increase over that of 1946, when this nation had just ended the most expensive war any nation ever engaged in. The interest paid each year on such a debt far exceeds the total income of many states. If a stable economy existed the interest on such a debt would probably be difficult to justify. However, the cost of construction of a school building over the same period has increased from $12 a square foot to $36 a square foot in some areas. The institution that overbuilt twenty years ago has had the use of its buildings for several years, and might not have been able to afford them at current prices. The total local-government indebtedness in 1966 was about $66.7 billion, of which $22.3 billion, or

33.4 percent of the total, was for schools.[6] So long as the seemingly continuous inflation of the U.S. economy continues, a school's bonds, if they can be sold for less than 5.5 percent (average rate of inflation for past three years), are excellent methods of financing educational plants. The appreciation of the buildings will more than exceed the interest paid to finance construction.

If a building program does not receive the benefit of appreciation by inflation, borrowing adds substantially to the price of a school building. Would it be wise to finance all construction on a pay-as-you-go basis? It is as difficult to get taxpayers, as it is homeowners, to pay for a building outright. They are generally unwilling to plan for tomorrow's expenses by budgeting present resources in a manner that would create a fund to be utilized at a later date. Benson explains that a pay-as-you-go system is rarely feasible despite its theoretical logic for evening out tax expenditures. Historically, he claims, reserve funds have been mismanaged and diverted to uses other than those for which they were created.[7]

If a school makes a decision to sell bonds in order to provide money for capital outlays, it should attempt to make its bonds as marketable as possible. Generally, the interest rate is low relative to other types of borrowing if the school district has an excellent credit rating. Both the federal government and some state governments have legislated concessions that make school bonds an attractive investment. Since the interest from school bonds is tax-free income, people with a large amount of money to invest can avoid paying income taxes on a major investment by purchasing such bonds. Several states, including Florida, New York, and Pennsylvania, have enacted legislation that protects a school-bond purchaser's investment. Such hierarchical commitments have resulted in large savings to local schools. The reader who has additional questions about this topic is encouraged to read Section C of Part Five of Benson's *Perspectives on the Economics of Public Education*.[8]

Table 4.4 clearly indicates that the public schools are borrowing more money each year, but it also shows that the percentage of the total expenditure for interest has been quite constant over the decade. If education is spending the same or a smaller percentage of its income each year, one might expect to have relatively stable interest rates over the decade, but such has not been the case. The data show clearly that the cost of borrowing has increased steadily (with one exception) over the decade. It appears that throughout the decade of the sixties and the early part of the

6. Ibid., p. 188.
7. Charles S. Benson, *Perspectives on the Economics of Public Education* (New York: Houghton Mifflin Co., 1963), p. 467.
8. Ibid., p. 374.

TABLE 4.4

INTEREST PAYMENTS ON PUBLIC SCHOOL (K–12) DEBT, 1961–70

School Year	Expenditures for Interest (in Millions of Dollars)	Percentage Increase over 1959–60	Total Expenditures (in Billions of Dollars)	Percentage of Total Expenditures for Interest
1961–62 . .	587.8	20.1	18.4	3.2
1962–63 . .	626.7	28.0	19.7	3.2
1963–64 . .	701.0	43.2	21.3	3.3
1964–65 . .	738.5	50.9	23.0	3.2
1965–66 . .	791.6	61.7	26.2	3.0
1966–67 . .	905.3	84.9	28.4	3.2
1967–68 . .	984.9	101.2	31.9	3.1
1968–69 . .	1,103.7	125.5	35.8	3.1
1969–70 . .	1,191.3	143.3	39.5	3.0

SOURCE: *Financial Status of the Public Schools, 1970* (Washington: National Education Association, Committee on Educational Finance, 1970), pp. 34, 35.

seventies a substantial portion (over 45 percent) of the capital outlay was caused by rising prices. Some educators feel that with the declining need for new instructional classrooms during the seventies, local school districts and colleges should attempt to reduce their outstanding indebtedness. If this were done, and inflation were curbed, there would be additional money to invest in promoting more effective instruction.

TABLE 4.5

INTEREST RATES ON SCHOOL BONDS, 1963–70

Year	High	Low
1963	3.31%	3.01%
1964	3.32	3.12
1965	3.56	3.04
1966	4.24	3.51
1967	4.45	3.40
1968	4.85	4.07
1969	6.90	4.82
1970	7.12	5.95

SOURCE: *Financial Status of the Public Schools, 1970* (Washington: National Education Association, Committee on Educational Finance, 1970), p. 46.

Investor confidence in the possibility of curbing inflation and in the security of school bonds is not evidenced in the spiraling cost of borrowing. Table 4.5 presents data relating to interest costs.

If a person could purchase income tax–exempt school bonds at 7.12 percent (the high for May 28, 1970) and reinvest the interest at the same rate, he could parlay $5 million into $40 million over a period of thirty years. The increase of $35 million on his investment represents how much money is paid out in interest by local school districts for which they receive no tangible goods.

SOCIETAL OPPORTUNITY COSTS

The last item to be discussed in analyzing the cost of providing education is one that in the future should and probably will increase the size of its bite of educational expenditures. Increasingly public schools, colleges, and universities are recognizing their responsibility to help people continue their education throughout their lives. An increasingly popular mission for educational institutions at all levels is to contribute to the life-long education of all citizens who ask for assistance. England is experimenting with the open university. Colleges and universities are emphasizing the opportunity for continuing and extension education. Public schools and community colleges are providing facilities and information for citizens who are nonmatriculating students. As people have more leisure, such programs should increase in number and scope. Making library and physical education facilities available to the public is frequently the forerunner of more extensive cooperation. Will those who utilize such services supply the additional funding necessary to provide, maintain, and supervise the services?

MARKETING OF EDUCATION

If educational institutions are to fulfill their role in society, they will increasingly have to utilize public relations and marketing practices that have been fruitful in the competitive world. The amount public institutions spend on advertising should probably be restricted. For them to be highly competitive in soliciting students would be very much like a husband and wife bidding against each other at a public auction. Public-institution operational resources should be utilized to improve services and designated raisons d'être. On the other hand, private institutions, which are forced to sell their services in a highly competitive market, must offer special options not available in public institutions in order to survive.

ACCESSIBILITY

Some of the factors that determine the accessibility of educational services are proximity to consumer, environment between consumer and educational institution, presence or absence of free or inexpensive transportation, entrance standards, and the cost of obtaining an education at a particular institution. In densely settled areas, it is generally economically feasible to build a K–12 school building within easy walking distance of pupils. Where the population is more scattered, most school systems provide buses. In 1968 over 17 million students were transported to school at public expense. The total cost for this service was nearly $1 billion.[9]

Many large housing-developers have either donated school sites or made a centrally located piece of property available at nominal cost. The builders know that easy accessibility to a school will increase the sales potential of their houses. Increasingly larger numbers of junior colleges are providing student bus transportation between the college and towns within 100 miles of the college. This enables students to live at home and commute daily. Many of the large urban universities are so sprawled out that bus service is provided between buildings on the campus and the contiguous student-housing areas.

Some sort of mass transportation may be utilized to partially thwart crime in the streets. A person may live relatively near an institution of learning, yet be fearful of walking to it because of the danger of an accident, assault, rape, or robbery. However, the existence of a freeway, a railroad, or a canal between a residential area and a school can be a safety hazard, especially for young children. In some metropolitan areas public schools are experimenting with the park plan. This plan provides easily protected walkways through educational parks that are free from motor vehicle traffic.

Private education is not available to many people because of its high cost. The soliciting of scholarship money and the provision of opportunities for employment of students attending a private institution can improve its accessibility to a broader cross-section of society. It is entirely possible and reasonable for a private institution to remain exclusive if it wishes. Public institutions can increase their accessibility by making an education available to people at all hours when called upon to do so, thereby making

---

9. *Statistical Abstract of the United States: 1971*, p. 120.

it possible for students to work for income during the day and attend college later in the evening. Tuition and other charges vary greatly from locality to locality, from state to state, and from one institution to another. For example, the cost of attending South Dakota State University or Texas A&M University is about $1,250 for a resident student, while for a resident student at the State University of New York at Stony Brook the fee is about $2,250 and at a private institution like Wesleyan University in Middletown, Connecticut, it is about $4,775.[10] In public schools there still exists a great deal of discrimination on how completely a student can participate in school activities. While the schooling is supposedly free, the student must provide funds for school materials and supplies, the school newspaper, the annual, athletic contests, plays, dances, club dues, and field trips. Students who lack sufficient money to meet such diverse demands cannot be full-fledged participants in all school activities.

Some institutions set entrance standards so high that they eliminate many potential students. Highly specialized training available only in private, exclusive secondary-level academies may be required to meet entrance requirements. The environment in which a person was reared might be responsible for language deficiencies that thwart his admission. Many institutions have established arbitrary "cut-off" scores on the Graduate Record Examination, thereby denying some persons access to graduate education. Some entrance standards have no substantial research to prove their merit. They are enacted because someone feels they might assure a higher level of competence among students, or in some cases they are merely used to keep out certain groups of people.

SALE PRICE OF EDUCATION

In modern times social institutions have increasingly turned over their responsibilities to the school. Sex, drug, and driver education were long the responsibility of the family but now have become part of the school curriculum. The seven cardinal principles of education put forth over fifty years ago are another example of schools' increasing responsibility.[11] Over a half-century ago schools were charged with the responsibility of helping students to become worthy citizens and providing the vocational education that would enable them to become wage-earners. The school has generally been willing to accept any new missions given to it, but these

10. *The Official Associated Press Almanac, 1973* (New York: Almanac Publishing Co.), pp. 377–96.
11. Edward W. Knight, *Fifty Years of American Education* (New York: Ronald Press, 1952), p. 105.

services must be paid for by someone. As schools assume responsibility for functions formerly the domain of other social institutions, the citizenry must stand ready to supply tax money to carry out the additional programs. In Minnesota and Texas, taxpayers receive a very large bargain in public education because of the foresight and integrity of their ancestors. Permanent school funds were created in these two states that are now worth several hundred million dollars in each case. The reader might well ponder whether action taken now could similarly alleviate school-tax burdens for future generations.[12]

The private sector of education has a far more tenuous position than the public institutions. Those in charge of private schools must constantly be aware of the resources they need to operate and how close these come to being paid for by the consumers. If private schools price their services too high they will drive away consumers, yet if they do not have sufficient resources to offer worthwhile programs they will soon lose the clientele they serve. Very few educational institutions are economically profitable operations, and many of them could not exist without the generosity of their alumni or the church or other outside support they receive.

This chapter has dealt with the cost of supplying education in the United States and has attempted to show how this expenditure has been increasing substantially both in magnitude and in percentage of gross income of taxpayers. Increased expenditures can be partially justified by the increasing responsibility of the schools. Are the educational institutions changing to meet the new demands placed upon them? Many taxpayers feel the schools are not sensitive enough to the needs of the people they serve. The rate of change probably increases each year and some social institutions must help people adjust to a changing environment. In higher education there is a definite movement toward permitting students to have more "say-so" in planning their degree programs. A strong plea is being made by patrons of the public school for it to serve more effectively the needs of the neighborhood in which it is located. The concept of accountability is likely to be a dominant theme for the seventies, and conscientious educators at all levels are beginning to examine more carefully their role in society.

There is a definite trend toward centralization in the field of professional education, as is evidenced by the growth of such organizations as the American Association of University Professors, the National Education Association, and the American Federation of Teachers. Will these new power blocs cope as effectively with their public responsibilities as they

---

12. Fletcher Harper Swift, *A History of Public Permanent School Funds in the United States, 1795–1905* (New York: Henry Holt & Co., 1911).

do with their responsibilities to their members in the educational profession? Will these groups become so engrossed in self-perpetuation that they lose sight of their larger responsibility to the society that permitted their emergence and sustains their existence?

In conclusion, there will probably be greater opportunities for professional education with each passing year. If the profession can effectively adjust its services to meet changing markets it should grow in numbers and stature. Hopefully education will police itself to become accountable, and will once again enjoy the public confidence and support it has enjoyed throughout most of its history.

BIBLIOGRAPHY

National Education Association, Committee on Educational Finance. *Financial Status of the Public Schools 1970.* Washington, 1970. Fifty-four-page book containing many informative tables about professional education in the United States, with limited pertinent comments by the committee about the tables. Annual report that should be consulted for statistical information on the profession, which is supplied on major cities and the fifty states and thus can be used in comparative studies. As reference source, should be rated excellent.

SWIFT, FLETCHER HARPER. *A History of Public Permanent School Funds in the United States, 1795–1905.* New York: Henry Holt & Co., 1911. If persons responsible for investing and perpetuating school funds in other states had been as effective and honest as those in Minnesota and Texas, public education would be much simpler to finance today. Swift gives state-by-state description of what funds were made available until the time he wrote and how they had been utilized. Very worthwhile historical document.

CHAPTER 5

Market versus Public Solutions to the Problems of Financing Education

As we noted in previous chapters, education is becoming increasingly costly both in absolute sums spent on it and also as a percentage of the gross national product. In our country, elementary and secondary education has generally been financed by property taxes at the local level. In recent decades, the expansion of public institutions in the higher education area has resulted in an increased tax burden on the population. This situation has caused a "taxpayers' revolt" against the mounting financial burden of education. These negative reactions have taken the form of the defeat at the polls of bond issues intended to expand education and of budget reductions or increases not in pace with increments in student populations. All this has brought about an "era of accountability" in education along with the accusation that many educational institutions have not in the past and are not now being operated on an efficient basis.

The purposes of this chapter are: (1) to define the current financing problem in education; (2) to describe and evaluate the various market-solution approaches being proposed; (3) to analyze the public-solution approach in terms of sources, magnitude, and areas of expenditures; (4) to briefly apply several economic principles to the problem; and (5) to present a brief summary and conclusion.

MARKET AND PUBLIC CONCEPTS

These new financial strains have resulted in various proposals intended to solve the problem of how best to finance education. Generally the recommendations made can be classified as "market solutions" or as "public solutions." It is important to note the decision-making process of these two approaches. The market approach is a private-economy effort while the public avenue becomes a public-economy way of providing desired educational services. The accompanying figure presents a pictorial sketch of the decision-making process in the two sectors. As the figure demonstrates, society starts with scarce resources and works toward satisfying human wants: in our case, the demand for education. The private approach, also referred to as the *market solution*, rests on individual decision-making. Scarcity of resources and the demand for these resources is reflected in the marketplace, where it is translated into a price. In education some of these prices are tuition, cost of books, food and lodging expenses for students. Here we have an exchange between buyers and sellers with the consumer trying to maximize his satisfaction and the seller attempting to operate in a cost-price relationship that will permit him to survive and continue in operation. Whether an individual can obtain the resources or the services he wants in the private sector depends on his ability to pay the going rate for the goods and services that he seeks. Private-sector prices must cover costs in the long run or the institution will cease to function.

In the public economy or *public-solution* approach, the scarcity of resources to satisfy human wants is the same as in the private sector. However, whereas supply and demand in the marketplace become the determinant of price in the private sector, in the public area the budget process serves this function. While values are assigned in the private economy by the willingness of individuals to purchase available goods and

RESOURCE ALLOCATION IN THE PUBLIC AND PRIVATE SECTORS

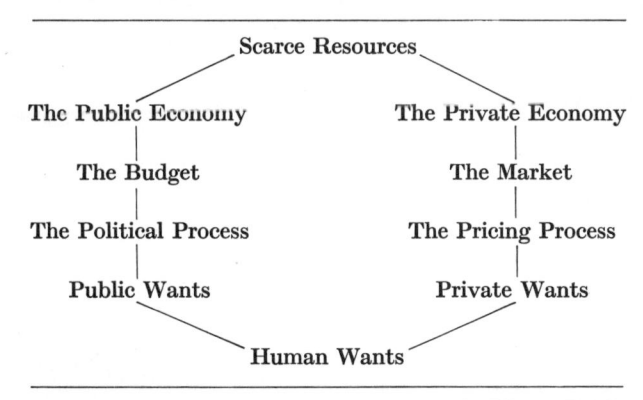

```
                    Scarce Resources
                   /                \
         The Public Economy      The Private Economy
                |                        |
            The Budget              The Market
                |                        |
        The Political Process      The Pricing Process
                |                        |
            Public Wants              Private Wants
                   \                /
                     Human Wants
```

SOURCE: Ansel M. Sharp and Bernard F. Sliger, *Public Finance* (Homewood, Ill.: Dorsey Press, 1964), p. 4.

services, in the public area the political process and budgets reflect the priorities of public officials. *The ballot box governs in the public-solution process while dollar-votes rule in the market-solution approach.* Because funds in the public sector are allocated through governmental agencies, services can be provided on the basis of need and costs can exceed the prices charged, which is not the case in the private sector. In carrying on overall economic activity, as is the case in education, there is considerable interaction between the public and private sectors. Government expenditures for public education involve taking resources from the private economy through taxation, either on a voluntary or an involuntary basis, and distributing them. This leaves fewer resources available in the private sector and thus has an impact on market prices.

The use of "market" and "public" approaches for some goods and services is quite clear. For example, there are *purely collective goods and services* that cannot be priced in the market because they cannot be divided into units small enough to permit pricing and thus do not lend themselves to a market solution. Examples of these items are national defense, air traffic control, food and drug protection. Another category is *private goods that are publicly supplied,* such as the utilities. In this case a *natural monopoly* situation normally exists where it is more efficient to have one rather than several suppliers. It would, for example, be quite inefficient to have two telephone companies servicing the same neighborhood because this would lead to needless duplication of poles and lines and would be quite costly. Again, society has resolved this problem by providing regulatory agencies that keep the monopoly power of these suppliers under some form of control.

Another group of goods and services, called *merit goods and services,* is provided free of charge or below market prices and is intended to elevate the economic standards of certain groups. Such action is justified by the goals of equitable treatment of individuals and improved distribution of goods and services. Examples are subsidies for public housing, public hospitals, and assistance programs for the needy who, for one reason or another, are unable to take care of themselves economically. Through the government sector this approach partly solves the problem of shifting resources from affluent members of society to those who are not affluent.

The case of education is complex because it falls into what economists call semicollective goods and services. These are goods and services that can be divided into smaller parts that can be priced and offered through the market or public areas. The nature of these types of goods or services is that society overall tends to benefit from them beyond the well-being that is received by the individual users. Thus, these types of goods or services stand between purely collective goods and services and those, representing the major part of economic activity in the United States, which are processed through the marketplace. Because of the fact that goods and services in this category can be provided either by the market or by the government, difficulties and conflicts tend to develop. It is in this context of being a semicollective good that much of our current controversy as to how education should be financed is taking place.

MARKET SOLUTION

The arguments against the current system of financing education are varied. One criticism is that in the public sector our schools tend to be monopolies, which do not offer the amounts and variety of education needed and are inefficient. Some people are of the opinion that if schools are to provide quality education at a low per unit cost, they must be brought under the influence of competitive forces in the free market. Presumably, in this situation parents and students would have some sovereignty by having the opportunity to select the area where they would spend their money. The logic is that if parents and students have a choice they will tend to go where they will get the most for their expenditure and in the process put pressures on educational institutions for improving the quality of education.

Specifically, there have been several ways suggested to execute free-market education in the United States. *Decentralization of school systems* has been espoused. This would presumably allow more influence to be felt from local areas and give the minority groups in large cities a greater voice in their educational system. The argument is that in the past monopolistic systems to a great degree disregarded the needs of the disadvantaged. Presumably, school districts would be brought under the control of leaders in the areas from where the majority of the student population is being drawn.

Some people, however, reason that such a system would not necessarily result in the kind of competition that improves quality. They argue that what would be done is simply to substitute a local monopoly, be it on a racial, ethnic, or economic level, for the overall monopolistic control that is now in existence. School systems would be fragmented, some *economies of scale* currently being realized might be lost, and the decentralization effort would thus be uneconomical. It is also felt that such decentralized systems might provide the means by which the undesirable biases and bigotries of each area would be given a large amount of influence over the type of education that the children receive. This situation would present problems to graduates later on because most of these youngsters would have to leave their home areas to find work in other locations where different cultural and social values prevail. Some teachers fear that a situation such as this will also place them under increasing local pressures and may thwart their efforts to conduct educational instruction in a professional manner. Parents who are not satisfied with decentralization in one area, while able legally to move to another region, may find that in reality moving is impossible for economic reasons. It is likely that in major metropolitan centers the better-quality schools would be unable to accommodate the large number of students who would probably wish to enroll. This situation again would not help to move lower-income minority groups into middle-income-type community schools.

One proposed solution would *give the buyer a choice* in the type of education by using tax money to establish both public and private schools. The private schools would be organized and geared to meeting the needs of particular minority groups in our nation. In a large metropolitan area, for example, we would have public schools run by the local government and private educational institutions under the control of different religious denominations and racial or ethnic groups. Public financial support to private schools would be determined on the basis of enrollment, levels of income in the area, or some other type of need. This recommendation would tend to decentralize the organization of schools and provide for competition. Also, this type of decentralization would be based on religious and racial affiliation rather than on geography. The competition that would result would revolve around ideological differences rather than the quality of education. Some people are of the opinion that such a system would promote and perpetuate segregation on racial and religious levels and would not stress the quality that is sought for in educational services.

Another proposed solution is the *voucher system*. The vouchers would be equivalent to what the locality spends per pupil in public schools, and each school would be reimbursed by the local government to the amount of the voucher. Proponents of this plan feel that it would promote healthy competition because schools would be placed in a situation where they would have to present clearly their overall programs and goals. If they did not live up to these stated objectives, they might be driven from the market. Also, parents would be free to select the school they think most desirable, regardless of whether it is public or private. Some advocate, along with this approach, "bonus" vouchers for disadvantaged students, which, they feel, might lead to the better-quality schools attempting to recruit these youngsters in an effort to obtain increased financial support. The opinion is held by some that the voucher system would give lower-income individuals a considerable range of choice in selecting an education, which would be about the same situation now being experienced by the middle class.

Opponents of the voucher approach feel that it might tend to promote and perpetuate racially segregated schools, which is counter to the stated objectives of our government. Some are of the opinion that this might result in public schools becoming a place where students would go only when not accepted in private schools. The use of public tax monies to support religious schools would violate the constitutional principle of separation of church and state. Finally, antagonists of this proposal feel that inferior schools might be established by individuals whose objective is to exploit the public's lack of knowledge about educational programs. However, some students of this issue argue that some of these objections could be overcome by setting student quotas on a racial basis and by establishing controls to reduce public subsidization of religious instruction per se. Also, accreditation standards could be established by each state and applied to all schools in general, thus reducing the danger of inferior programs being set up by individuals solely interested in profit-making.

Finally, some argue that the answer is to provide educational services through a *performance contract*. An educational institution would indicate what it would like to have done in its program or programs, and put it out for bids to organizations that would attempt to meet these needs. In such a situation it would be expected that competition would be enhanced because organizations would come into existence to provide these services. Presumably, better technology and educational materials would be made available; furthermore, cost pressures would be present and would tend to lead to greater efficiency. One of the problems with this approach is measuring the results of such programs. For the moment, many skills defy accurate measurement, and this obstacle is a major hurdle which has as yet not been overcome.

In summary, one of the difficult dimensions of cost-pricing in education is the realization that society as a whole gains from the education of a person. As we have already stated, education is critical in productivity and economic growth, and can bring returns in excess of cost to the total economy. Furthermore, education has other side-benefits. For example, educated people are less likely to commit crimes, which, as we know, involve economic costs. Also, they are less likely to wind up on the welfare rolls, which have become a heavy tax burden on society. From a political point of view, it is extremely questionable whether a system such as ours can survive without an enlightened citizenry.

PUBLIC SOLUTION

Public education has more and more become dominant in our nation and along with this increasing importance of the public sector in education has come a rapid acceleration in financing burdens. Table 5.1 presents a breakdown of financial resources for education in selected years. The data are in billions of dollars and omit expenditures for schools of nursing not affiliated with colleges and universities. The major observable trend from 1960 to 1971 is the increasing role of the federal government as a source of funding. In 1960, 6.9 percent of total expenditures in education were obtained from the federal government, and by 1971 this figure had increased to 11.7 percent. An accompanying component of this development is the decline in the amount of support obtained from local governments, from 39.3 percent in 1960 to 32.9 percent in 1971. The percentage of state and all other sources has stayed remarkably constant from 1960 to 1971. Several other developments are of interest. In the area of higher education, support which came from the federal sector increased from 14.9 percent in 1960 to 20.6 percent in 1971. The "all other" category experienced a decline from 58.2 percent in 1960 to 52.6 percent in 1971. Federal support to private institutions of higher education rose from 17.0 percent in 1960 to 24.9 percent in 1971. Overall, total dollar expenditures for education in the United States increased by $50.6 billion from 1960 to 1971, which represented an increase of 205 percent.

Table 5.2 presents both public and private school expenditures in millions of dollars, by amounts and percentages and by type of control and level of instruction, in selected years from 1930 to 1971; prior to 1950 Alaska and Hawaii are excluded. Expenditures excluded from these data are those for schools of nursing not affiliated with colleges and universities, higher education current outlays for auxiliary enterprises in other non-educational concurrent expenses, and expenditures for residential schools for exceptional children. Included are expenditures for federal schools for Indians and federal schools on federal installations that are not part of the breakdown. These data reveal that the national commitment to education has been considerable. *A significant figure is the increase of expenditures as a percentage of the gross national product from 3.1 in 1930 to 7.7 percent in 1971.* The percentage of the total going for public education has remained rather stable, being 82.1 in 1930 and 81.3 percent in 1971.

Table 5.3 represents revenue and expenditures for public elementary and secondary schools for selected years 1950 to 1968. Data are in millions of dollars and percentages, and expenditures for 1950 exclude Alaska and Hawaii. "Other sources" represent intermediate and local sources and include receipts from gifts and tuition, and transportation fees paid by patrons. "Instruction expenditures" include salaries of clerical assistants, free textbooks, school-library books, and supplies. "Other current expenditures" represent outlays for summer schools, adult education, community colleges, and, starting in 1960, community services. "Capital outlays"

TABLE 5.1
Amount and Source of Public and Private School Expenditures, 1960–71

Item	Total 1960	Total 1966	Total 1969	Total 1970	Total 1971	Percentage 1960	Percentage 1966	Percentage 1969	Percentage 1970	Percentage 1971
Total	24.7	45.4	62.0	70.6	75.3	100.0	100.0	100.0	100.0	100.0
Federal	1.7	5.1	7.3	8.0	8.8	6.9	11.2	11.8	11.3	11.7
State	7.2	13.1	18.5	21.1	22.5	29.1	28.9	29.8	29.0	29.0
Local	9.7	15.0	20.2	23.6	24.8	39.3	33.0	32.6	33.4	32.9
All other	6.1	12.2	16.0	17.9	19.2	24.7	26.9	25.8	25.4	25.5
Public	19.7	35.3	49.9	57.3	61.2	100.0	100.0	100.0	100.0	100.0
Federal	1.2	3.7	5.4	5.9	6.5	6.1	10.5	10.8	10.3	10.6
State	7.2	13.0	18.4	21.0	22.4	36.6	36.8	36.9	36.6	36.6
Local	9.7	15.0	20.2	23.6	24.8	49.2	42.5	40.5	41.2	40.5
All other	1.6	3.6	5.9	6.8	7.5	8.1	10.2	11.8	11.9	12.3
Private	5.0	10.1	12.1	13.3	14.1	100.0	100.0	100.0	100.0	100.0
Federal	0.5	1.4	1.9	2.1	2.3	10.0	13.9	15.7	15.8	16.3
State	z	0.1	0.1	0.1	0.1	z	1.0	0.8	0.7	0.7
Local	z	z	z	z	z	z	z	z	z	z
All other	4.5	8.6	10.1	11.1	11.7	90.0	85.1	83.5	83.5	83.0
Elementary and secondary schools	18.0	30.2	39.9	45.7	48.1	100.0	100.0	100.0	100.0	100.0
Federal	0.7	2.2	2.9	3.0	3.2	3.9	7.3	7.3	6.6	6.6
State	5.6	9.6	13.1	15.1	16.0	31.1	31.8	32.8	33.0	33.3
Local	9.5	14.6	19.6	22.8	24.0	52.8	48.3	49.1	49.9	49.9
All other	2.2	3.8	4.3	4.8	4.9	12.2	12.6	10.8	10.5	10.2

(continued)

TABLE 5.1 (*continued*)

Item	Total					Percentage				
	1960	1966	1969	1970	1971	1960	1966	1969	1970	1971
Public	15.9	26.5	35.7	41.0	43.3	100.0	100.0	100.0	100.0	100.0
Federal	0.7	2.2	2.9	3.0	3.2	4.6	8.0	8.1	7.3	7.5
State	5.6	9.6	13.1	15.1	16.0	35.4	36.3	36.7	36.9	37.0
Local	9.5	14.6	19.6	22.8	24.0	59.6	55.2	54.9	55.6	55.3
All other	0.1	0.1	0.1	0.1	0.1	0.4	0.5	0.3	0.2	0.2
Private, all other	2.1	3.7	4.2	4.7	4.8	100.0	100.0	100.0	100.0	100.0
Institutions of higher education	6.7	15.2	22.1	24.9	27.2	100.0	100.0	100.0	100.0	100.0
Federal	1.0	2.9	4.4	5.0	5.6	14.0	19.1	19.9	20.1	20.6
State	1.6	3.5	5.4	6.0	6.5	23.9	23.0	24.4	24.1	23.9
Local	0.2	0.4	0.6	0.8	0.8	3.0	2.6	2.7	3.2	2.9
All other	3.9	8.4	11.7	13.1	14.3	58.2	55.3	53.0	52.6	52.6
Public	3.8	8.8	14.2	16.3	17.9	100.0	100.0	100.0	100.0	100.0
Federal	0.5	1.5	2.5	2.9	3.3	14.9	17.6	17.5	17.8	18.2
State	1.6	3.4	5.3	5.9	6.4	41.4	38.4	37.0	36.4	35.8
Local	0.2	0.4	0.6	0.8	0.8	4.6	4.1	4.5	4.5	4.4
All other	1.5	3.5	5.8	6.7	7.4	39.1	39.9	41.0	41.3	41.6
Private	2.9	6.4	7.9	8.6	9.3	100.0	100.0	100.0	100.0	100.0
Federal	0.5	1.4	1.9	2.1	2.3	17.0	22.1	23.4	24.1	24.9
State	z	0.1	0.1	0.1	0.1	1.5	1.2	1.2	1.2	1.2
Local	z	z	z	z	z	0.2	0.1	0.3	0.3	0.3
All other	2.4	4.9	5.9	6.4	6.9	81.3	76.3	75.1	74.4	73.6

z = Amount less than $500,000.
SOURCE: *Statistical Abstract of the United States: 1971*, p. 103.

TABLE 5.2

CONTROL AND LEVEL OF INSTRUCTION OF PUBLIC AND PRIVATE SCHOOL EXPENDITURES, 1930–71
(In millions of dollars)

Control and Level of Instruction	1930	1940	1950	1960	1965	1969	1970	1971, est.
Total	3,234	3,200	8,796	24,722	40,200	62,000	70,600	75,300
Percentage of gross national product	3.1	3.5	3.4	5.1	6.4	7.2	7.6	7.7
Current expenditures and interest	2,700	2,833	7,229	20,003	33,200	53,100	61,300	65,800
Capital outlay or plant expansion	534	367	1,567	4,120	7,000	8,900	9,300	9,500
Public	2,656	2,697	7,057	19,447	31,000	49,900	57,300	61,200
Percentage of total	82.1	84.3	80.2	78.7	77.1	80.5	81.2	8.13
Current expenditures and interest	2,233	2,376	5,767	10,139	25,700	42,500	49,300	53,000
Elementary and secondary	1,969	2,106	4,869	12,951	20,100	31,000	35,900	38,100
Higher	237	270	898	3,131	5,600	11,500	13,400	14,900
Capital outlay or plant expansion	423	321	1,290	3,308	5,300	7,400	8,000	8,200
Elementary and secondary	371	258	1,014	2,662	3,700	4,700	5,100	5,200
Higher	52	63	276	622	1,600	2,700	2,900	3,000
Private	578	503	1,739	5,275	9,200	12,100	13,300	14,100
Current expenditures and interest	467	457	1,462	4,464	7,500	10,600	12,000	12,800
Elementary and secondary	200	205	654	1,993	3,000	3,700	4,100	4,200
Higher	267	252	808	2,471	4,500	6,900	7,900	8,600
Capital outlay or plant expansion	111	46	277	812	1,700	1,500	1,300	1,300
Elementary and secondary	37	25	136	419	500	500	600	600
Higher	74	21	141	393	1,200	1,000	700	700

SOURCE: *Statistical Abstract of the United States: 1971*, p. 102.

TABLE 5.3

REVENUES AND EXPENDITURES OF PUBLIC ELEMENTARY AND SECONDARY SCHOOLS, 1950–68
(In millions of dollars and percents)

Item	1950 Total	1950 Percentage	1960 Total	1960 Percentage	1964 Total	1964 Percentage	1966 Total	1966 Percentage	1968 Total	1968 Percentage
Revenue, total	5,437	100.0	14,747	100.0	20,544	100.0	25,357	100.0	31,903	100.0
Federal sources	156	2.9	652	4.4	897	4.4	1,997	7.9	2,806	8.8
State sources	2,166	39.8	5,768	39.1	8,078	39.3	9,920	39.1	12,276	38.5
Other sources	3,116	57.3	8,327	56.5	11,569	56.3	13,440	53.0	16,821	52.7
Expenditures, total	5,838	100.0	15,613	100.0	21,325	100.0	26,248	100.0	32,977	100.0
Current	4,723	80.9	12,462	79.8	17,646	82.7	21,702	82.7	27,744	84.1
Day schools	4,687	80.3	12,329	79.0	17,218	80.7	21,053	80.2	26,877	81.5
Administration	220	3.8	528	3.4	745	3.5	938	3.6	1,249	3.8
Instruction	3,112	53.3	8,351	53.5	11,750	55.1	14,445	55.0	18,376	55.7
Plant operation	428	7.3	1,085	6.9	1,446	6.8	1,763	6.7	2,075	6.3
Plant maintenance	214	3.7	423	2.7	539	2.5	624	2.4	790	2.4
Fixed charges	261	4.5	909	5.8	1,344	6.3	1,701	6.5	2,388	7.2
Other services	452	7.7	1,033	6.6	1,394	6.5	1,583	6.0	2,000	6.1
Other current	36	0.6	133	0.9	428	2.0	648	2.5	866	2.6
Capital Outlay	1,014	17.4	2,662	17.0	2,978	14.0	3,755	14.3	4,256	12.9
Interest	101	1.7	490	3.1	701	3.3	792	3.0	978	3.0

SOURCE: *Statistical Abstract of the United States: 1971*, p. 120.

prior to 1966 exclude expenditures by state and local school-housing authorities. The data reveal that federal funding increased from 2.9 percent of the total in 1950 to 8.8 percent in 1968. The increase in federal funds was accompanied by a percentage decline in "other sources" from 57.3 percent in 1950 to 52.7 percent in 1968. Expenditures for instruction increased from 53.3 percent in 1950 to 55.7 percent in 1968, and those for plant operation declined from 7.3 to 6.3 percent from 1950 to 1968. A significant development is the decline in the percentage spent for capital outlays, from 17.4 in 1950 to 12.9 in 1968.

Table 5.4 presents new bond sales for public school purposes from 1958 to 1970. The data are in millions of dollars and rates of interest. Information is for the fiscal years ended during the stated years and covers bonds sold for construction of public elementary and secondary school facilities. Several observations become apparent. School districts are by far the most important issuing agencies and in 1970 represented 59.5 percent of total bond sales. The total amount remained relatively stable during the three years, decreasing from $2.9 billion in 1968 to $2.8 billion in 1970. A significant development was the sharp rise in interest rates from an average of 4.57 percent in 1968 to 6.39 percent in 1970.

Table 5.5 presents estimated public school expenditures for 1971, and personal income for 1969, by state in millions of dollars. Total expenditures include interest on the school debt, which is not shown separately. The "other programs" category refers to expenditures for summer schools, adult education, community services, and community colleges and technical institutes under the jurisdiction of local boards of education. School expenditures under the per capita category are based on the resident-population estimates of the Bureau of the Census as of April 1, 1970. Personal-income estimates were obtained from the Office of Business Economics in the *Survey of Current Business*, August, 1970. An x in the table indicates that the data are not applicable in this case, and a z refers to amounts of less than $500,000. In some instances, states share rank. For example, Illinois and Michigan both rank fourteenth in expenditures per pupil in average daily attendance. Also, Arizona and Nevada both rank twenty-second and New Mexico and Florida twenty-eighth in the same category. In order to have the lowest rank equal to the number of states presented, the numbers fifteen, twenty-three, and twenty-nine are omitted. The average expenditure per pupil in average daily attendance for the District of Columbia represents an estimate, and for Alaska it should be reduced approximately one-fourth to make it comparable to the amounts for other states.

The leading states in terms of average expenditures per pupil are

TABLE 5.4
New Bond Sales for Public School Purposes, 1968–70

Issuing Agency	1968 Sales Number	1968 Amount (millions of dollars)	1968 Average Net Interest Cost	1969 Sales Number	1969 Amount (millions of dollars)	1969 Average Net Interest Cost	1970 Sales Number	1970 Amount (millions of dollars)	1970 Average Net Interest Cost
All agencies	1,722	2,917	4.57%	1,529	2,904	4.88%	1,309	2,813	6.39%
State	6	167	4.25	3	16	4.02	14	188	6.22
County	60	170	4.43	48	160	4.64	85	220	6.43
City, town, township	135	381	4.45	93	244	4.70	112	287	6.38
School district	1,399	1,823	4.56	1,260	2,032	4.83	1,001	1,673	6.36
Authority	122	376	4.94	125	452	5.32	97	445	6.58

Source: *Statistical Abstract of the United States: 1971*, p. 120.

TABLE 5.5
Estimated Public School Expenditures, 1971, and Personal Income, 1969, by State

State	Current Expenditures					Per Capita			
	Total Expenditures	Elementary and Secondary Schools	Other Programs	Average per pupil in average daily attendance		Capital Outlay	School Expenditures (in dollars)	Personal income	
				Total (in dollars)	Rank			Amount (in dollars)	Rank
U.S.	44,424	36,454	1,573	858	x	5,061	219	3,637	x
N.E.	2,426	2,091	55	893	x	192	205	4,076	x
Maine	207	175	4	763	32	23	209	3,054	35
N.H.	138	106	z	729	34	23	181	3,471	26
Vt.	118	108	z	1,061	4	8	266	3,247	32
Mass.	1,118	938	45	856	21	85	197	4,156	8
R.I.	193	164	1	983	7	21	203	3,858	13
Conn.	656	600	5	997	6	32	216	4,595	1
M.A.	9,600	7,955	337	1,174	x	976	258	4,155	x
N.Y.	5,157	4,336	217	1,370	2	452	283	4,442	4
N.J.	1,727	1,530	29	1,088	3	110	241	4,241	7
Pa.	2,715	2,089	91	948	12	414	230	3,659	17
E.N.C.	8,884	7,330	179	876	x	1,087	221	3,928	x
Ohio	2,034	1,750	30	778	27	200	191	3,738	15
Ind.	1,164	861	17	770	31	241	224	3,687	16
Ill.	2,420	1,968	87	937	14	291	218	4,285	6
Mich.	2,292	1,879	34	937	14	295	258	3,994	11
Wis.	974	872	12	977	8	60	220	3,632	19

(*continued*)

TABLE 5.5 (continued)

State	Total Expenditures	Current Expenditures: Elementary and Secondary Schools	Current Expenditures: Other Programs	Current Expenditures: Average per Pupil in average daily attendance Total (in dollars)	Current Expenditures: Average per Pupil in average daily attendance Rank	Capital Outlay	Per Capita: School Expenditures (in dollars)	Per Capita: Personal income Amount (in dollars)	Per Capita: Personal income Rank
W.N.C.	3,587	2,956	133	845	x	404	220	3,497	x
Minn.	1,102	896	13	1,021	5	151	290	3,635	18
Iowa	721	590	31	944	13	87	255	3,549	23
Mo.	835	686	62	747	33	67	179	3,458	27
N.Dak.	110	98	2	689	36	7	178	3,012	38
S.Dak.	131	113	—	713	35	16	196	3,027	37
Nebr.	270	214	8	683	37	40	182	3,609	20
Kans.	419	360	17	771	30	36	186	3,488	25
S.A.	5,963	4,917	120	748	x	780	194	3,287	x
Del.	160	117	z	954	10	35	292	4,107	9
Md.	1,042	808	8	968	9	191	266	4,073	10
D.C.	180	142	11	1,046	x	28	238	4,722	x
Va.	954	810	20	800	25	100	205	3,307	30
W.Va.	271	238	3	624	45	27	156	2,603	47
N.C.	848	713	54	642	41	67	167	2,888	42
S.C.	458	392	8	656	39	50	177	2,607	46
Ga.	769	656	15	634	43	70	168	3,071	34
Fla.	1,279	1,040	—	776	28	213	188	3,525	24
E.S.C.	1,778	1,546	37	560	x	145	139	3,651	x
Ky.	462	404	1	621	46	42	143	2,847	43
Tenn.	577	510	9	601	47	40	147	3,808	44
Ala.	435	370	2	489	50	51	126	2,582	48
Miss.	304	263	25	521	49	12	137	2,218	50

W.S.C.	3,351	2,824	30	667	x	392	173	3,060	x
Ark.	279	240	3	578	48	27	145	2,488	49
La.	698	621	1	806	24	55	192	2,781	45
Okla.	429	385	3	676	38	35	168	3,047	36
Tex.	1,946	1,578	23	636	42	275	174	3,259	31
Mt.	1,834	1,549	21	767	x	220	221	3,328	x
Mont.	169	142	5	866	20	19	243	3,130	33
Idaho	133	110	z	629	44	16	186	2,953	40
Wyo.	83	76	—	927	17	6	250	3,353	29
Colo.	467	399	5	780	26	50	211	3,604	21
N.Mex.	251	209	6	776	28	34	247	2,897	41
Ariz.	406	333	—	808	22	66	229	3,372	28
Utah.	216	185	3	643	40	24	204	2,997	39
Nev.	108	95	2	808	22	7	222	4,458	3
Pac.	7,002	5,286	660	891	x	865	264	4,164	x
Wash.	836	665	60	873	19	85	245	3,848	14
Oreg.	475	411	1	935	16	53	227	3,573	22
Calif.	5,347	3,943	590	879	18	665	268	4,290	5
Ala.	142	106	2	1,429	1	31	471	2,460	2
Hawaii	202	162	7	951	11	32	263	3,928	12

x = Data not applicable in this case.
z = Amount less than $500,000.
SOURCE: U.S. Department of Health, Education, and Welfare, *Fall 1970 Statistics of Public Schools.*

Alaska, New York, New Jersey, Vermont, and Minnesota. In terms of school expenditures as a percentage of personal income, the leading five states by rank are Connecticut, Alaska, Nevada, New York, and California. If the Alaska figure is adjusted by the 25 percent recommended by the Department of Health, Education, and Welfare, Office of Education, then New York leads the nation in average expenditure per pupil with the sum of $1,370. This should be contrasted with Alabama, which is spending an average of $489 per year and ranks fiftieth among all the states. These data vividly reveal the problem of providing equitable educational services on a nationwide basis.

Table 5.6 presents data on how education has fared in forty state appropriations for selected years between 1962 and 1972. These data reveal that state support for *higher education* has been rising more rapidly than total state revenue. Between 1967 and 1972, state revenues increased by 67 percent while appropriations for higher education jumped 87 percent. During the same period, higher education's share of state revenues increased from 14 percent to 16 percent. Overall, total expenditures for education rose by 59 percent; however, education's share of state revenues dropped from 53 to 51 percent. Considerable differences in the share of education and the percentage of all education funds originating from state sources can be noted, the highest being Louisiana with 85 percent and the lowest Connecticut with 32 percent.

Table 5.7 presents enrollment data and federal expenditures for work and training programs administered by the U.S. Department of Labor from 1963 to 1970. Enrollment opportunities refers to the number of training positions provided for by funding and, as can be noted, federal obligations for these types of programs increased from $796 million in 1967 to $1.4 billion in 1970. The most important source of funds was the Manpower Development and Training Act and institutional training was the largest type of program. Enrollment data for the Concentrated Employment Program are excluded because individuals often enrolled in one or more program components. JOBS refers to Job Opportunities in Business and the Job Corps program was transferred to the Department of Labor as of July, 1969.

Table 5.8 presents, in millions of dollars, a summary of federal funds for education and related activities from 1966 to 1971. The data include Puerto Rico and outlying areas and represent "obligational authority" through 1967 and outstanding outlays in capital thereafter. As can be noted from the data totals, grants and loans increased by 58 percent from 1966 to 1971. Of the total expenditures, elementary-secondary education, higher education, and vocational-technical and continuing education received 35.6, 40.8, and 20.0 percent respectively during 1971. In terms of

TABLE 5.6
STATE APPROPRIATIONS FOR EDUCATION, 1962-72

	Colleges' % Share of Total Appropriations						All Education's % Share of Total Appropriations						Colleges' % Share of Education Appropriations					
	1962–63	1967–68	1968–69	1969–70	1970–71	1971–72	1962–63	1967–68	1968–69	1969–70	1970–71	1971–72	1962–63	1967–68	1968–69	1969–70	1970–71	1971–72
Ala.	12	19	19	18	18	21	78	83	83	81	80	79	16	23	22	22	22	26
Ariz.	16	25	27	23	25	27	55	66	66	74	69	72	29	38	41	31	36	37
Ark.	14	17	17	17	18	17	57	67	66	65	64	60	25	25	26	26	27	28
Calif.	16	15	16	19	20	17	62	53	52	55	55	46	25	28	32	34	36	38
Colo.	21	23	25	25	26	30	54	55	53	51	57	64	39	43	46	48	46	47
Conn.	6	12	11	12	11	10	30	42	38	37	34	32	19	29	30	32	33	38
Fla.	14	20	18	19	21	19	x	69	80	75	76	68	21	29	23	26	27	28
Ga.	9	8	12	12	13	14	41	61	64	66	64	64	x	13	18	18	20	21
Hawaii	8	11	10	12	12	14	44	48	46	46	44	49	19	23	22	26	27	29
Ill.	16	21	23	21	17	18	44	53	53	50	45	48	36	41	43	43	39	38
Ind.	20	19	22	21	20	21	73	68	76	72	62	68	27	28	28	29	32	32
Iowa	21	24	23	21	22	22	41	45	51	51	52	52	51	54	41	41	42	42
Kans.	21	23	25	25	23	23	52	64	64	63	63	61	41	35	36	39	36	38
Ky.	10	17	18	17	18	19	61	65	66	64	67	69	16	27	27	27	26	28
La.	15	19	18	18	23	19	93	90	84	84	x	85	16	21	22	21	23	22
Maine	x	x	x	x	x	x	36	40	47	43	46	43	x	x	x	x	x	x
Md.	18	16	17	17	16	18	59	54	52	48	52	47	30	30	32	35	32	38
Mich.	x	14	13	14	14	13	70	34	33	36	36	34	26	41	40	40	38	39
Miss.	x	x	x	x	x	x	x	x	64	46	49	63	x	x	x	x	x	x
Mo.	x	x	18	20	20	20	x	x	58	58	57	57	x	x	31	33	35	34
Nebr.	22	17	16	19	19	18	22	17	29	35	32	30	x	x	56	54	58	61
Nev.	x	x	x	x	x	x	71	74	65	69	65	69	x	x	x	x	x	x
N.J.	4	6	6	6	6	6	22	27	30	29	30	28	20	22	18	20	21	23
N.Mex.	x	x	15	16	16	17	x	x	73	74	73	71	x	x	21	21	22	23
N.Y.	8	12	11	12	13	13	48	49	50	47	45	46	17	24	23	26	28	29
N.C.	7	12	13	15	15	17	64	62	61	62	62	64	11	20	22	24	24	27
N.Dak.	25	24	28	28	25	25	70	54	60	60	54	54	36	45	47	46	47	47
Ohio	9	11	14	15	16	16	47	51	51	52	50	50	18	21	27	29	31	31
Okla.	29	28	30	25	26	29	71	67	67	68	68	71	40	42	44	37	39	40
Oreg.	20	29	29	28	28	29	59	59	59	56	56	58	34	49	49	50	50	49
Pa.	5	9	12	13	13	12	46	51	47	52	51	51	11	18	25	25	24	22
R.I.	x	x	x	x	x	x	28	34	32	35	38	48	x	x	x	x	x	x
S.C.	7	6	10	11	11	12	59	61	59	60	56	55	12	16	16	18	19	21
S.Dak.	26	35	32	34	29	29	38	57	52	54	59	52	68	61	62	62	58	56
Tenn.	12	17	19	19	19	19	78	79	80	76	79	78	16	21	23	25	24	25
Utah	11	16	17	15	16	17	64	58	61	55	58	60	17	29	28	27	28	28
Vt.	13	13	15	16	12	13	39	42	52	52	45	46	32	30	29	31	27	27
Va.	14	19	24	19	20	17	63	71	92	73	73	69	22	27	26	26	33	31
Wash.	x	19	30	23	21	29	x	62	64	68	64	64	x	31	44	33	39	40
W.Va.	14	13	16	17	16	15	56	48	53	55	59	51	25	27	29	30	28	28

x = Data not available.

SOURCE: "How Education Has Fared in State Appropriations," *Chronicle of Higher Education* (Washington, D.C.), April 16, 1973, p. 6. (For additional information see Lyman A. Glenny and James R. Kidder, *Preliminary Report on State Financing of Education*, Berkeley Center for Research and Development, Education Commission of the States.)

TABLE 5.7
FEDERAL WORK AND TRAINING PROGRAMS, 1963–70

Program	Enrollment Opportunities (In Thousands)					Federal Obligations (In Millions of Dollars)				
	Total, 1963–70	1967	1968	1969	1970	Total, 1963–70	1967	1968	1969	1970
Total	5,019	808	824	911	972	5,229	796	802	1,030	1,360
Manpower Development and Training Act, total	1,599	271	230	199	201	2,008	298	296	273	316
Institutional training	982	126	124	111	122	1,609	215	218	208	246
On-the-job training	583	145	99	78	64	379	83	75	59	60
Part-time and other training	33	z	8	10	16	19	z	4	6	10
Neighborhood Youth Corps, total	2,888	513	533	540	492	1,651	349	282	321	308
In school	763	139	135	101	97	NA	67	59	49	59
Out of school	397	79	63	50	45	NA	148	96	122	98
Summer	1,725	294	339	387	350	NA	133	127	148	151
Work Training in Industry	3	z	1	2	—	NA	z	z	1	—
Operation Mainstream	50	8	11	14	18	138	24	22	41	51
Public Service Careers	47	4	3	6	34	129	16	8	18	87
Special Impact	7	4	1	1	—	10	7	2	1	—
Concentrated Employment Program	162	8	32	53	69	498	78	93	114	187
JOBS (federally financed)	245	—	10	99	136	437	24	90	161	162
Work Incentive Program	22	—	10	99	136	189	—	9	101	79
Job Corps	22	x	x	x	22	170	x	x	x	170

— Represents zero. NA = Not available. x = Not applicable. z = Less than $500,000.

SOURCE: U.S. Department of Labor, *1971 Manpower Report of the President*, p. 299.

TABLE 5.8

FEDERAL FUNDS FOR EDUCATION AND RELATED ACTIVITIES, 1966–71
(In Millions of Dollars)

Type of Support, Level, and Program Area	1966	1967	1968	1969	1970	1971
Federal Funds Supporting Education in Educational Institutions						
Total grants and loans	6,780	8,353	7,804	8,055	9,237	10,708
Grants	6,168	7,411	7,201	7,523	8,631	10,117
Elementary-secondary education	2,480	3,038	2,967	2,833	3,212	3,605
School assistance—federally affected areas	434	469	506	308	656	512
Economic opportunity and Indian education programs	404	721	629	552	534	574
National Defense Education Act—equipment, guidance	104	109	109	74	59	47
Supporting services	173	274	280	290	238	232
Assistance for educationally deprived children	959	1,057	1,057	1,096	1,208	1,459
Teacher Corps	7	11	16	19	18	27
Vocational education	185	195	185	152	181	236
Dependents' schools abroad	86	88	68	109	137	145
Public lands revenue for schools	54	50	52	66	82	80
Assistance in special areas	69	57	58	71	79	171
Veterans education	—	1	3	5	6	11
Emergency school assistance	—	—	—	—	—	100
Other	5	5	2	5	13	14

(continued)

TABLE 5.8 (continued)

Type of Support, Level, and Program Area	1966	1967	1968	1969	1970	1971
Higher education	2,830	3,634	3,263	3,318	3,830	4,367
Basic research in educational institutions proper	940	1,033	1,062	1,021	991	1,033
Research facilities	194	251	200	239	235	198
Training grants	366	364	381	405	844	891
Fellowships and traineeships	265	350	320	248	191	196
Facilities and equipment	669	822	549	482	374	350
Other institutional support	164	170	140	173	178	231
Other student assistance	214	591	609	740	1,004	1,457
Other assistance	19	55	2	10	13	11
Vocational-technical and continuing education	857	939	971	1,367	1,589	2,146
Vocational, technical, and work training	818	827	852	1,163	1,269	1,686
Veterans education	6	54	80	124	245	401
General continuing education	19	29	29	60	66	48
Training state and local personnel	14	29	11	19	9	11
Loans, higher education	612	742	603	532	606	591
Student loan program, National Defense Education Act	236	238	226	260	295	382
College facilities loans	376	504	377	273	311	209

Other Federal Funds for Education and Related Activities

	3,904	3,930	3,606	3,340	3,426	4,036
Total						
Applied research and development	1,027	1,088	1,142	1,237	1,234	1,347
School lunch and milk programs	422	448	544	598	676	965
Training of federal personnel	1,707	1,537	1,138	640	692	737
Professional training, military	1,625	1,443	1,065	546	676	723
Civilian education and training in non-federal facilities	82	94	73	94	15	15
Library services	86	141	136	186	170	186
International education	233	327	272	278	193	244
Educational exchange program	54	45	42	38	31	34
Agency for International Development projects	112	203	140	170	111	170
Peace Corps and other education and training	67	79	90	70	51	39
Other	430	388	373	400	460	556
Agricultural extension service	91	93	90	97	125	160
Educational television facilities	15	3	7	9	19	28
Education in federal correctional institutions	4	6	4	4	5	6
Other education and training	39	54	47	54	53	69
Surplus personal property transferred, acquisition cost	266	216	199	224	246	279
Surplus real property transferred, fair value	15	17	26	13	12	14

SOURCE: *Statistical Abstract of the United States: 1971*, p. 135.

percentage increases, the vocational-technical and continuing education group experienced the sharpest rise with an increment of 150 percent. During 1971, the federal government spent over $4 billion for education in related activities. The major area of expenditures under this grouping was applied research and development with $1.3 billion. School lunch and milk programs amounted to $965 million; training of federal personnel, $737 million; surplus personal property transferred, $279 million; and international education, $244 million. There was a reduction of $549 million in 1968 compared to 1967 in the volume of grants and loans and the curtailment of $324 million during the same year of federal funds for education in related activities. This is accounted for by cutbacks in the federal budget resulting from a rising federal deficit, which increased from $8.7 billion in 1967 to $25.2 billion in 1968. Additionally, inflationary pressures were present and the Consumer Price Index rose from 100.0 in 1967 to 104.2 in 1968.

Table 5.9 presents data on vocational programs that received federal assistance for selected years between 1950 and 1969. The data are in thousands and include Puerto Rico for all the years, the Virgin Islands starting in 1955, and Guam commencing in 1960. The total number of students in these programs increased by 137 percent from 1950 to 1969. The largest number enrolled in 1969 was in secondary education, with 4.1 million out of the 8.0 million being in this area. Home economics was the program that attracted the largest number of students. Total expenditures in these programs amounted to $1.4 billion and the federal government spent $255 million or 18.6 percent of the total.

The data in the tables reveal a clear picture. Our nation is spending an increasing amount of money for education. With the increase in the size of the population, the increment in the percentage of our population completing a larger number of years in schools, plus inflationary pressures, which are driving up all types of costs, taxpayers face an ever-increasing burden. This situation, coupled with student unrest on some campuses, has led taxpayers to resist increasing resource allocations for education. Also, it has brought educational operations under closer scrutiny in terms of how efficiently resources are being managed. The suspicion is held by some that we may be overeducating or improperly educating many of our people. The United States has led the way in the mass-education approach with a great deal of success; however, we are now at a point where the stresses and strains of numbers and pressures on resources are bringing the whole operation under question and rigorous examination. Given this situation, what do economic principles suggest concerning a possible solution?

TABLE 5.9
FEDERALLY AIDED VOCATIONAL PROGRAMS, 1950–69

Item	1950	1955	1960	1965	1966	1967	1968	1969
Students, Total	3,365	3,314	3,763	5,431	6,070	7,048	7,534	7,979
Adult	NA	NA	NA	2,379	2,531	2,941	2,987	3,050
Secondary	NA	NA	NA	2,819	3,048	3,533	3,843	4,079
Other	NA	NA	NA	233	491	574	704	850
Type of program:								
Home economics	1,430	1,432	1,588	2,099	1,898	2,187	2,283	2,449
Office occupations	—	—	—	731	1,238	1,572	1,736	1,835
Trades and industry	805	871	938	1,088	1,269	1,491	1,629	1,721
Agriculture	765	776	796	888	907	935	851	851
Other	365	235	445	626	758	862	1,025	1,123
Teachers[a]	NA	NA	NA	123	124	133	147	167
Full-time	NA	NA	NA	54	64	72	80	91
Part-time	NA	NA	NA	70	81	81	90	103
Expenditures, Total (mil. dol.)	129	165	239	605	800	1,004	1,193	1,369
Federal (mil. dol.)	27	30	45	167	234	260	262	255
Percent of total	20.7	18.4	19.0	26.0	29.2	25.9	22.0	18.6
Type of program								
Home economics (mil. dol.)	37	49	60	98	113	125	161	181
Office occupations (mil. dol.)	—	—	—	54	92	133	176	217
Trades and industry (mil. dol.)	48	56	73	145	186	236	229	318
Agriculture (mil. dol.)	39	54	67	87	89	103	110	118
Other (mil. dol.)	5	6	30	221	320	407	517	535

[a] Includes duplication. — represents zero. NA = Not available.
SOURCE: *Statistical Abstract of the United States: 1971*, p. 133.

ECONOMIC PRINCIPLES AND EDUCATION

One of the major problems we face in applying economic concepts to education is the measuring of the results of education. Who is to say that a student attending a university where it costs $3,000 per year to educate him necessarily receives a better education than one going to an institution where the expenditure is $2,000? Also, it is extremely difficult to measure the benefits that accrue to society as a whole from training an individual; that is, as we have previously enumerated, benefits deriving from reductions in unemployment, the crime rate, and welfare expenditures. With all this in mind, there are certain economic concepts that should be utilized in formulating an answer to the current financial crisis in education.

A key criterion to be applied in the expansion of educational facilities is *per unit costs*. As long as the expansion of facilities is not increasing real cost per student, expansion of physical facilities and new campuses may be carried on in an efficient manner. However, when costs per unit are driven up considerably, the situation must be closely evaluated. *The forecasting of student demand* for educational services is a critical starting point in the overall decision-making process. A key factor affecting demand is the question of how far our educational institutions should move into proximity with students as compared with moving the students to the educational institution? Somewhere in the answer to this question lies an *optimum point of locating a facility* in relation to student accessibility. The point is that in recent times we have seen the development of major universities in large cities, which represents a movement to take education to the students as opposed to having students go considerable distances to attend universities, as was the case in the past.

Once the demand component has been estimated and a proximity factor determined, the problem of how to supply educational services with efficiency must be considered. To assist in this effort it is necessary to introduce the enrollment of a particular institution, teacher-student ratio, and the possible substitution of capital for labor in the teaching process. The demand for educational services can be influenced through higher costs, proximity factors, and also the availability of programs.

The educational component must keep in mind that the rapidly changing character of demands for educational services reflects the changing needs of our society. Thus, programs ought to be flexible, with new ones introduced as the demand develops and old ones phased out as the need for them subsides. A reduction in the number of programs in some institutions will probably be beneficial to the efficiency process. Because of the rather inflexible nature of many of our educational institutions, programs are at times continued beyond the point of reasonable use to society. Cost of production per student on a yearly basis thus must be determined *for different levels of enrollment utilizing available technology*. It will be impossible in a given situation to have all programs at the same level of efficiency. Therefore, a situation must be developed where combinations of several programs can be established and a total package of efficiency for an institution determined. André Daniere in his book *Higher Education in the American Economy* suggests sectioning-off the nation into geographical areas. Thus, once an optimum size is determined for a given university with a given set of programs, one can determine where to locate the next educational institution in the geographical area it is to serve.

If education were a business operating for profit, the marketplace would make these decisions and educational institutions would be run on the principle of *long-run profit maximization*. Currently in our educational process there is competition. However, this competition often takes the form of efforts to attract high-quality students and thus may result in costly services. It is not the kind of competition that is likely to result in efficiency and cost reduction. Efforts to reduce per unit costs, when they have come about, as in the last few years, have usually been the result of legislative pressures because of the previously enumerated resource scarcities. In providing an educational mix, it appears that the private sector in education is facing the problems of private enterprise in general, because just as business has experienced increasing government controls so has the greatest growth in education taken place in the public sector. Our nation must continually determine how much of the taxpayers' funds should be channeled into the support of private education. This not only gets involved in constitutional questions, but also in cost factors in terms of how much is saved by having private institutions supply some educational services which are financed out of private funds. Overall, the pressures to apply *cost-benefit analysis* to educational expenditures will increase. Hopefully, the tools to quantitatively measure the social benefits of educational services will be improved.

SUMMARY AND CONCLUSIONS

In summary, education is facing several critical problems. The cost of providing educational services in the United States is reaching such a high level that taxpayers are becoming increasingly resistant to augmented educational expenditures. Confronted by extremely rapid changes in technology and in the economy's skill-needs, our educational institutions are often finding it difficult to maintain the flexibility essential to providing the required trained manpower.

The matching of the demand for educational services and the supply of educational services is difficult to achieve because of the dynamic nature of our economy. Consequently, at times we see the spectacle of pronounced shortages in some fields while at the same time college graduates are unable to find jobs in other occupations because of an oversupply. In an effort to find a solution to the financial aspects of the situation, there has been much discussion of the controversial question of "market" versus "public" solutions to education problems. Because education is a semi-collective service it can be provided by either the private or the public sector, and this has resulted in considerable controversy.

One of the major dilemmas faced in the financial dimensions of education is measuring the direct and indirect benefits of education. It would appear that our nation will continue to closely examine the type of education provided, and in all probability in the near future will continue the trend toward supporting vocational and applied types of education. Educational institutions will increasingly be run on a business basis, with cost-benefit analysis at the forefront of the decision-making process. Organizationally, we are likely to encounter new forms that will provide educational institutions with greater flexibility to adjust to the needs of the economy. More latitude will probably be forthcoming in the use of taxpayers' funds for private education in order to provide savings for society through the utilization of facilities and other resources made available by the private sector. Educational technology, which has had rather limited application, is likely to be expanded and become a means of providing more lower-cost education for a larger number of people.

BIBLIOGRAPHY

Carnegie Commission on Higher Education. *The More Effective Use of Resources: An Imperative for Higher Education.* New York: McGraw-Hill Book Co., June 1972. Study covering financial crisis, behavior of costs, student retention, faculty efficiency, professorial salaries, potential unionization, budgets, and innovation in higher education. Planning for capital expenditures and overall analysis of effective use of resources is undertaken. Good source for those interested in looking at financing of education from managerial point of view.

Committee for Economic Development. *Education for the Urban Disadvantaged: From Pre-school to Employment.* New York: Research and Policy Committee of CED, March 1971. Pages 49–74 cover instructional systems and facilities, new approaches, accountability, control, and equalizing of school resources. Analyzes these areas and presents some possible solutions to major problem in higher education today: education of disadvantaged in cities.

DANIERE, ANDRÉ. *Higher Education in the American Economy.* New York: Random House, 1964. Comprehensive coverage of higher education on American economic scene. While very few data are presented, author analyzes American higher education in terms of economic principles. Good book for those who have high degree of interest in economics and how this discipline may help in analyzing financing of higher education.

McFARLANE, WILLIAM H., and WHEELER, CHARLES L. *Legal and Political Issues of State Aid for Private Higher Education.* Atlanta: Southern Regional Education Board, 1971. Thorough study of legal and political dimensions of higher education, particularly as they apply to South. However, has value for those studying legal issues facing higher education in our nation as a whole. Basic question covered, what kinds and amounts of public support to private institutions are possible with existing legal and political regulations?

CHAPTER 6

Summary and Conclusions

Educational institutions at all levels are facing a great economic challenge caused by the financial crisis currently besetting the United States. Furthermore, the pressure to provide "relevant" education is great, and the defining of what is "relevant" is causing considerable difficulty. Part of the financial squeeze has arisen from the American effort to educate the masses, and taxpayers today are questioning all phases of the education process and are demanding accountability.

Education is an industry and is thus subject to economic principles as are other industries. One of the difficulties faced in applying business-management devices to the operation of educational institutions has been the problem of measuring the indirect contribution of education to the economy. While the direct economic benefits of education outlays are easily measured, the indirect contribution to the economy is difficult to ascertain. In 1971, education was responsible for expenditures amounting to 7.7 percent of the gross national product. Furthermore, the education industry makes an important contribution to productivity, which is a key variable in increasing overall real wages and controlling inflation. Some researchers are of the opinion that education is the most important factor in the economic growth process. In an era when change is an everyday problem faced by industry, education helps to give individuals the flexibility to adapt to new job demands.

In an effort to provide expanding college-level training in special vocational and technical areas and to meet higher education demands, the community college, which is generally located within a close geographical distance to its students' residences, has been introduced and is an American innovation. More recently, the multicampus university located in urban centers is another effort to take education to the consumer, rather than the consumer to education as was the case in the past. This type of university has built-in laboratories in the communities it serves. Adult education programs are reaching millions of people who had never been considered part of the education market. Education is now more and more being viewed as a life-long process that does not have to take place in a formal institutional setting. Examples are public library services, educational television, and programs like "Continental Classroom." As more students enroll in educational programs, the costs of providing these services are rising rapidly and taxpayers are reacting negatively to these new financial demands.

The increased demand for educational services is the result of various developments. Minorities, including women, are availing themselves of higher education in greater numbers than they did in the past. Our economy, with its constantly increasing demand for higher-skilled individuals, is looking to educational institutions for its supply of efficient employees. Human obsolescence, resulting from rapid changes in technology, is further increasing the demand for educational services. Furthermore, government financial-assistance programs of various types make it possible for more people to continue in school at all levels of the spectrum than was the case in the past.

In supplying educational services it appears that the education industry has not increased its productivity to keep pace with efficiency improvements in other areas of the economy. The application of technology to the educational process has been inadequate. Student-teacher ratios, which are at least a quantitative measure of productivity, have not changed in approximately the past fifty years. Obsolescence of equipment and building facilities is a problem that besets educational institutions as well as other economic units. Physical-plant expansion has taken a large sum of money in the past three decades, and rising interest rates have made the financing of educational facilities more expensive. Inflation is having an adverse impact on educational operations just as it has negatively affected many other sectors of the economy. A more critical problem is the obsolescence of educational programs and faculty.

The questions of standards and the quality of educational services supplied is an ever-present and continuing one. Public education is increasing its share of the education market because private educational institutions, due to their inadequate financial resources, are finding it more difficult to compete. Society is increasingly considering the opportunity-costs of longer periods of education for its members, more so than it did in the past. The education services offered by the public schools have been directed into controversial areas, such as sex, drugs, and driver education, which in the past were considered to be the responsibility of the family.

The achieving of a balance between the demand for and supply of educational services in the United States is difficult. This has led at times to over- and under-supplies of educational services of various kinds. The issue of a market versus a public solution to providing needed services is difficult to resolve because education is a semicollective service that can be provided by either the public or the private sector of the economy. At present, it appears that the general public is more disposed to supporting vocationally oriented education than was the case in recent years.

What measures should educational institutions in the United States undertake to meet their current economic problems?

1. Institutions will have to be increasingly operated on business-management principles. This means cost-benefit analysis, planned program budgets, and better forecasting techniques. Purchasing and marketing devices will have to be utilized. Society and individuals will increasingly consider the opportunity-costs of education services. No doubt, the application of business know-how to the management of educational institutions will be made difficult by the complex nature of providing education services, which tend to be rather diverse and, as we have indicated, somewhat difficult to measure in terms of quality.

2. The organizational structure of educational institutions will have to be made more flexible. With the rapidly changing skill-needs of the economy, these institutions will need to introduce new programs and phase out obsolete ones with a minimum of bureaucratic red tape. Thus it may be that the current trend toward organizing institutions on a program basis, as opposed to departments and divisions, may be a fruitful undertaking.

3. More use will have to be made of available technology in the educational process. The resistance of faculty and administrators to applying technology in instructing individuals will have to be overcome.

4. Better productivity measures for educational output must be developed. Some quantification of the subjective aspects of the indirect contribution of education to the economy must be developed. When this is done, educational operations must increase their productivity as measured by these new standards. Ways for faculty members to handle efficiently large numbers of students need to be devised. This will probably result from greater application of technology and new instructional materials.

5. Care will have to be taken not to overinvest or underinvest in some areas of education. Failure to achieve this goal will mean having otherwise capable but inadequately trained individuals frustrated by their inability to find employment, and seeing the economy face a shortage of trained manpower.

6. It is likely that economies will be realized if public funds are used to partially support private education in nonreligious areas. If properly handled, this approach may reduce the financial burden on the taxpayer because part of the costs of education would be underwritten by private

individuals. For example, some private institutions have excellent physical plants, equipment, and library collections.

7. The creating of new educational institutions will increasingly have to come under economic scrutiny. It is becoming clear that taxpayers in some areas are unwilling or unable to support the increased number of such institutions.

8. Efforts must be made to eliminate obsolete programs and faculty. Periodic reviews of both programs and teaching and administrative personnel should be instituted.

9. Society will have to clarify for educational institutions the role they are to play. The current issue of vocational training versus liberal arts experience is of paramount importance and is causing a great deal of concern to decision-makers in educational institutions. A closer exchange must be developed between educational institutions and society as a whole. Educational institutions should always be aware of the practical realities of the needs of society. On the other hand, society deserves to benefit from the utilization of the know-how that is available in educational institutions in its efforts to solve a multitude of complex problems.